the CRY

the Desperate

Prayer that Opens

the Heart of God

keith
HUDSON

DESTINY IMAGE® PUBLISHERS, INC.
P.O. Box 310, Shippensburg, PA 17257-0310

"Speaking to the Purposes of God for This Generation and for the Generations to Come."

This book and all other Destiny Image, Revival Press, MercyPlace, Fresh Bread, Destiny Image Fiction, and Treasure House books are available at Christian bookstores and distributors worldwide.

For a U.S. bookstore nearest you, call 1-800-722-6774.
For more information on foreign distributors, call 717-532-3040.
Or reach us on the Internet: www.destinyimage.com.

ISBN 10: 0-7684-2825-4
ISBN 13: 978-0-7684-2825-4

For Worldwide Distribution, Printed in the U.S.A.

1 2 3 4 5 6 7 8 9 10 11 / 13 12 11 10 09

DEDICATION

This book is dedicated to the church that is searching for a deeper prayer life and longing to see a global move of God.

ACKNOWLEDGMENTS

My heartfelt thanks to my wife, Mary, for putting this book together;

To Ronda Ranalli at Destiny Image for saying that this is a kairos moment when God is longing to hear the heart-cry of the Church;

To pastors and spiritual mentors who have been a blessing in my life: Dr Mark Barclay, Mark Hankins, Pastor David Shearin, Dr. Stephen Johnson, Pastor Roger Brewer, Dennis Tinerino, and Pastor Randy Landis, to name a few;

To my mother, Ann Hudson, for all your love;

To Angela, my oldest daughter, the organizer and leader of the tribe;

To Katy, the singer, whose voice is created to worship, and to David, the missionary, with the heart of a lion;

To my sister Jan, who is among a great cloud of witnesses cheering me on, and her daughter, Jennifer, still here on earth walking toward her calling;

Thank you for your love and encouragement.

CONTENTS

PREFACE

Out of the depths have I cried to You, O Lord. Lord, hear my voice; Let Your ears be attentive to the voice of my supplications. If You, Lord, should keep account of and treat [us according to our] sins, O Lord, who could stand? But there is forgiveness with You... that You may be reverently feared and worshiped. I wait for the Lord, I expectantly wait, and in His word do I hope. I am looking and waiting for the Lord more than the watchmen for the morning, I say, more than watchmen for the morning. O Israel, hope in the Lord! For with the Lord there is mercy and loving-kindness, and with Him is plenteous redemption. And He will redeem Israel from all their iniquities (Psalm 130:1-8 AMP).

Sometimes situations in your life can seem so dark that only a cry will do. When it seems as if the midnight hour has come in your life, a midnight cry can be the beginning of a breakthrough.

Of course, midnight can be a time of intense darkness or gloom. But make no mistake: what midnight represents in Bible terms is a period of time halfway between dark and the breaking of a new day. Midnight *is* the middle of the night, but midnight also leads to the dawning of a new day.

Many are in the midst of a midnight season; many of God's people are desperate to hear from Heaven at this hour. They have had their hopes deferred and have waited a long time for the fulfillment of His promises to them. There is a cry that has been brought forth from their hearts during this period of brokenness, a time in which spiritual leaders, morality, and finances have fallen in front of their eyes.

With all of these challenges and with many still waiting for the answers to their prayers to be made manifest, there is nothing left inside but a cry: a desperate cry for a living God who hears and answers them suddenly and personally.

This may be your story; your cry may be the one I describe. Don't quit praying, because when you realize that God has heard your prayer (from the very first day you prayed), faith will arise in your heart. Be encouraged: He will answer your cry.

Your cry is a powerful force building within. Like a volcanic eruption produced when the pressure of the lava has reached its peak, or the shakings of an earthquake when the seismic plates underground are forced to shift, a cry comes out of the depths of your spirit to the Lord, the only Person who can help you in a midnight hour.

The Lord never leaves you nor forsakes you. Yet, those dark nights of the soul, when you feel like you are flying the plane of life instrument-rated, may cause you to wonder, *Where is God in all of this?* Fortunately, the Word of God is there to put you back on track; even so, some situations seem so extreme that only a cry from your heart will release the pressure valve.

When His peace returns to you and your spirit can agree

with His Word, life returns to normal. But sometimes, extreme circumstances require extreme action. The psalmist explains, "Lord, if You counted up our sins, none of us would make it" (see Ps. 130:3). Fortunately, He is a God of mercy; He is there for us, regardless of what we have done, always extending us the opportunity to repent and turn back to Him. He is ready to forgive you. This psalm underscores that, as we expectantly wait and trust Him to move, *"He will redeem Israel from all their iniquities"* (Ps. 130:8 AMP).

But first there has to be a cry.

What is a cry? What makes it so different from an ordinary prayer? When you cry, you "utter loudly...proclaim publicly"[1] or make "a loud exclamation."[2] In other words, your cry is not a passive whisper; it is a warlike shout to an almighty God. Webster's Revised Unabridged Dictionary defines *cry*: "To make a loud call...or exclaim vehemently...to shout; to vociferate; to proclaim; to pray; to implore."[3] Webster's gives an example from Matthew 27:46, which describes the last hours of the crucifixion: *"And about the ninth hour, Jesus cried with a loud voice...."*

But here is where the cry from the Holy Spirit comes in: it means: "To cry to, to call on in prayer; to implore. To proclaim; to name loudly."[4] A cry is "a loud or vehement sound, uttered in weeping, or lamentation; it may be a shriek or scream."[5] It is also defined as "a loud voice in distress, prayer or request; [an] importunate call."[6] Cries can be "bitter complaints of oppression and injustice."[7]

There is protection in the cry. The children of Israel had been complaining about wandering around in the wilderness and having only manna to eat. This complaining was a form of speaking against God; it was an open rebellion the Lord could not tolerate. So He sent fire among the worst ones and consumed those on the edge of the camp (see Num. 11:1). When they repented and cried to Moses, Moses prayed to the Lord for them and judgment was stayed.

Provision and sustenance come from a cry. The Bible says that He gives food to the young ravens that cry (see Ps. 147:9).

There is a warning in the cry: *"Go and cry in the ears of Jerusalem..."* (Jer. 2:2). God is commanding Jeremiah to rebuke His holy city. It is always wise to listen to God's rebukes. He uses prophets who will obey Him unconditionally to warn cities and nations who have gotten out of alignment with God's plan for them.

You don't have to be famous or wealthy to get God's attention. He will hear anyone whose heart is open before Him. *"When He maketh inquisition for blood, He remembereth them: He forgetteth not the cry of the humble"* (Ps. 9:12). God says He will avenge the injustices committed against you; He will eventually punish all oppressors and criminals. It is only through patience in that period of waiting for justice that you will possess your soul (see Luke 21:19).

The cry can also put an end to a desperate situation. In Isaiah 5:7, the Lord says that His vineyard is *"the house of Israel"* and *"the men of Judah His pleasant plant."* He said He expected to harvest good grapes of justice and righteousness. But instead this vine of the nation of Israel produced oppression and injustice until a great cry of mercy came up to Him and judgment came.

God has to allow what we allow; He is a God of mercy, but if we continually allow evil to reign in our lives, He is forced to withdraw and allow judgment to come. *"...I am the Lord, and no one else [is He]. I form the light and create darkness, I make peace [national well-being] and I create [physical] evil (calamity); I am the Lord, Who does all these things"* (Isa. 45:6-7 AMP).

If you translate this into the Hebrew, the verb *create* is used in the Hopal conjugation, meaning "caused to allow." In other words, the Lord has to allow what we as human beings allow here on earth. Consider Matthew 18:18: *"... and whatever you permit and declare proper and lawful on earth must be what is already permitted in heaven"* (AMP). He can't stop us from sinning or missing the mark; we are free moral agents. We must make the decision to line up our wills with His will. Yes, His Holy Spirit hovers over us and prompts us to make good choices (especially as we pray); but He will never force His way on us. While the devil desires to drive us; the Holy Spirit simply leads.

A holy God cannot join Himself with anything unholy; oil and water do not mix. Let your cry open the heavens; watch Him come down and rescue you in every situation. All it takes is for you to open your mouth wide with passion and holy fire and pour out your heart to Him.

A CRY TAKES YOU FROM RELIGION TO RELATIONSHIP

We have reached a point in Christianity where prayers by rote will no longer meet the need. Our prayers must be passionate and fervent, not polished and pristine.

> *"The earnest (heartfelt, continued) prayer of a righteous man makes tremendous power available [dynamic in its working]"* (James 5:16 AMP).

God wants to hear from your heart a prayer that is more than information recited from a printed page. The prayer God wants to hear is birthed from the revelation that resides in your soul!

I believe we are nearing the end of an age. Time as we know it is wrapping up. God is doing a quick work and needs to hear exactly what is burning in our hearts. He is not looking for a torrent of unnecessary words; the more direct and precise our prayers are, the more crystal clear our results will be.

Jesus is our perfect example. He did not belabor His final prayer on the cross. He simply said, *"Father, forgive them, for they know not what they do"* (Luke 23:34 AMP). His time was short; so is ours. It's time to get down to brass tacks. You have been taught; you may have been discipled in weekly Bible studies. You may have attended church and read your Bible diligently. But what is the message engraved upon your heart? What is the Lord speaking to your soul at this critical hour in history?

This is not a time to back down or be passive. It is time to cry out to the Lord with all of our hearts. He is looking for heroes in this last hour, people who will not be afraid to speak, live, and declare truth, even when the truth is unpopular.

Are you willing to stand up and speak for Him? Will you refuse to be intimidated by the faces people make when you say what you believe? Will you resist the temptation to be politically correct when others pressure you to conform? Are you willing to walk away from dirty jokes and pornography in the office; will you reject sexual advances or harassment even if it means losing a promotion? Will you cry out for the rights of unborn children, molested preschoolers, and abused women? Or will you fall in line with the crowd because it's easier not to ruffle their feathers?

In the end, the question is always the same: *Will you fear man or will you fear God?* When Judgment Day comes, will the record show that you lived His way or followed the world?

It's not too late to prepare for a strong finish. Now is the time to gear up our prayer lives, our speaking, and our think-ing. Realize that much more will be required of us in this last hour. We must be bold in our faith, not shrinking back from the Word of God, but proceeding with confidence in Him.

Throughout history, that kind of holy boldness has made great faith heroes out of ordinary men and women. God is ready to do the same today. Time is winding down, but He is not finished with us—not yet!

CHAPTER ONE

GOD HEARS
YOUR CRY

Most of our prayers result from a sense of obligation or originate from our own knowledge base. But God wants us to cry out to Him from a deeper place.

When God begins to put a cry in your heart, you will start to see things through His eyes. But, before a cry forms inside of you, you must begin to recognize the cry that originates in *His* heart.

We need to cry for our nation, our president, our school districts, our families, our children, and our churches. We need to cry for our troops and all they endure for our freedom. We need to pray and weep before the Lord for the right people to take public office.

We live in a society whose conscience has been seared by a hot iron. We come before the Lord with our books and our notes, but God wants to hear our hearts. We have become so smooth and sophisticated that our hearts have become cold. Too often, we don't really mean what we pray. But when we weep, there is, in our tears, a release!

There is coming a new depth in your prayer life and God wants to prepare you for it. But you must yield to the wooing of the Holy Spirit and let go of robotic and rigid prayers.

Because the conscience of so many is seared, few things move the average person. Even tragedy often fails to register on the heart, unless the tragedy is personally experienced. It is as though constant exposure to television, movies, and other forms of media and entertainment have made us callous to evil and the suffering of others.

There are so many voices out there, but only one voice is worth listening to. *"There are, it may be, so many kinds of voices in the world, and none of them is without signification"* (1 Cor. 14:10). It is the Lord's voice that makes the difference. He is the One who wants to put that cry back in you.

This is our midnight hour. Moses faced just such a time. He turned to God in that most critical point in his life: The Red Sea was in front of him, six million complaining Jews surrounded him, and Pharaoh's army was behind him. At the point where the Israelites stood, the Red Sea was 12 miles wide and 75 to 100 feet deep. Pharaoh's army threatened their very lives and charged them from the rear.

These Egyptians comprised a mighty host. There were 600 chariots in the king's guard (which was the pride of Egypt, according to the first-century historian Josephus). Pharaoh also assigned 50,000 horsemen and 200,000 footmen to wipe out the children of Israel.[1] No wonder the Israelites *"were sore afraid"* (Exod. 14:10).

At that point, Moses cried out to God, who immediately answered him, saying:

Wherefore criest thou unto Me? Speak unto the children of Israel, that they go forward: but lift thou up thy rod, and stretch out thine hand over the sea, and divide it: and the children of Israel shall go on dry ground through the midst of the sea (Exodus 14:15-16).

The Lord was, in effect, telling Moses, "I am not the one to help you in this situation. You are going to have to take authority and part the sea by yourself." Or, in other words: "I am not stretching out My hand; You are going to have to stretch out *your* hand." The fact remains, Moses' cry did get the Lord's response, even if it did not elicit the reaction Moses wanted.

God was essentially telling Moses that unless he played a part in his own deliverance, God could not help him. God had already brought Israel out of Egypt with all kinds of supernatural signs and wonders—everything from swarming locusts...to the Nile turning to blood...to thousands of children dying, including Pharaoh's own son.

But now Moses had to hold up the rod of authority and watch the Red Sea part. He already knew God could do it. But now Moses was being required to demonstrate God's power. God was not going to intervene for him this time. Nothing would happen until Moses took the first step.

What happened when Moses cried out to God? The Lord gave him an immediate answer. He told Moses to take action. Moses believed His words and obeyed Him. He didn't try to figure out how the multitude was going to get delivered from Pharoah's army. He didn't mull over logistics or try to understand details. How could he even have had the time to consider that a column of Israelites 400 people wide would need a path 1200 feet wide to cross the Red Sea? Not to mention the fact that this column of six million Jews would be eight and a half miles long.

There was not a moment to analyze the situation. Moses knew he must only believe God's voice and act on His words. That is what we must do in a crisis. Don't question *how* God is going to do what needs to be done; just cry out to Him, believe He will fight your battles for you, and get on with His instructions.

What if Moses had remained silent at this vital turning point, this historical moment when Israel was about to be freed from hundreds of years of oppression? What if he had buckled under the pressure of the cruel Egyptian army that was hard on his heels or surrendered to their hostility? Israel might never have become a nation. But no, Moses kept on moving in this place of trouble, suffering, and responsibility. He did not stand still in terror at the circumstances, even though it was surely the most terrifying situation Moses had ever encountered.

Habakkuk describes the kind of trust Moses demonstrated:

> *The Lord God is my Strength, my personal bravery and my invincible army; He makes my feet like hinds' feet and will make me to walk [not to stand still in terror, but to walk] and make [spiritual] progress upon my high places [of trouble, suffering, or responsibility]!* (Habakkuk 3:19 AMP).

When Moses finally cried out and lifted his rod over the Red Sea, the Lord actually dried up the sea floor, which moments before had been covered with water. Then the Lord blew a strong eastern wind which literally froze the 75- to 100-foot walls of water on either side of the Israelites as they marched through the sea.

> *And with the blast of Thy nostrils the waters were gathered together, the floods stood upright as an heap, and the depth were **congealed** in the heart of the sea* (Exodus 15:8, emphasis added).

The word, *congeal*, in the Hebrew is *qapha*, meaning to "thicken; freeze or congeal."[2] The thickened waters stood up as if frozen into solid ice. No one, not even Moses, could have imagined that deliverance would occur in this way.

A KING CRIES OUT TO GOD

Finally—a king in the book of Second Chronicles who did everything right! So many of King Asa's predecessors only fulfilled half or three quarters of what the law required to reinstate the children of Israel's relationship with the Lord. But Asa actually commanded the people to seek the Lord and to obey the law and the commandment (see 2 Chron. 14:4).

He started by getting rid of their idols. When that happened, the land started to prosper again.

> *And he built fenced cities in Judah: for the land had rest, and he had no war in those years; because the Lord had given him rest. Therefore he said unto Judah, Let us build these cities, and make about them walls, and towers, gates, and bars, while the land is yet before us; because we have sought the Lord our God, we have sought Him, and He hath given us rest on every side. So they built and prospered* (2 Chronicles 14:6-7).

He assembled two armies totaling over half a million men. You would have thought King Asa was going to be able to turn the whole country toward God without any opposition.

Have you ever felt that way? You seem to have it all together: you have dedicated your whole life to God; you have raised your children in the ways of the Lord; you have a good marriage and everything seems to be working out. Then, all of a sudden, the enemy hits you with a sidewinder missile you never expected. That's exactly what happened to Asa. Just as he got his kingdom in place, the king of Ethiopia decided to wage war against him—out of the blue —with a million men and 300 chariots to boot!

Asa's army was outnumbered two to one. These were not good odds and he knew it. What would he do now? Just sit there and whine about it? What would you do? Would you tell the Lord all the things you have done right in your life? Would you remind God of what a good person you are and how many hours you've spent volunteering in children's church? Or would you ask, "God, how could You allow this to come upon me?"

Asa's attitude was none of the above. He knew his Maker. He *knew* the faithfulness of God, and he knew God was not his problem. Asa knew the Lord was His very present help in time of trouble.

> *And Asa **cried** unto the Lord his God, and said, Lord, it is nothing with Thee to help, whether with many, or with them that have no power: help us, O Lord our God; for we rest on Thee, and in Thy name we go against this multitude...* (2 Chronicles 14:11).

In other words, Asa was saying, "It doesn't matter how many troops I have or how many troops the king of Ethiopia has. You are still on the throne and You can turn this situation around." God heard Asa's cry and honored it; He could see that Asa was trusting Him first and foremost, no matter how bad the situation looked.

Still, Asa had to make the first move and release a heart cry that pierced the heavens straight to the throne of God. Asa pleaded for help, he exercised his faith, rested upon God's goodness, and took action. He went to war against an enemy despite insurmountable odds. The Lord heard his cry, smote the Ethiopians before Judah, and caused the battered forces to flee to Gerar. They were so soundly defeated they could not recover themselves to fight another battle. The Ethiopians didn't even try to come against Israel for another 300 years.

A CRY BETWEEN LIFE AND DEATH

For a man named Guy Wolek, a cry stood between his decision to live or die. Guy's life was spared when he cried out to the Lord in a church basement. He was on his way to commit suicide and had never heard the words, *"If thou shalt confess with thy mouth the Lord Jesus, and shalt believe in thine heart that God hath raised Him from the dead, thou shalt be saved"* (Rom. 10:9).

Raised all his life as a Catholic in Chicago, Illinois, Guy had made peace with his parents before going off to take his own life. He didn't tell them he was planning to go down a dark alley in downtown Chicago and kill himself.

But as Guy walked past a Catholic church, something prompted him to stop and go inside. Someone had once told him that if he would just ask Jesus to come into his life, Jesus would help him. So Guy decided he would take one last step of faith before ending it all. He walked into the church and said, "Jesus, if You are real, I need to have You in my life."

At that moment, God spoke to Guy's heart saying, "Guy, everything is going to be OK." The young man had been arrested in the Spirit. He bent his head over the church pew, crying and cussing at the same time. But when he got up from that place he felt like a new man. He had heard from God and his life had been spared. He knew he had changed: he could sense it in his heart.

Guy accepted the Lord that day, and it started by him pouring out his heart to God on the way to killing himself. Instead of ending his life, he had a new life. Within six months, Guy was filled with the Holy Ghost and totally delivered from alcoholism and drug addiction. He became involved in a Spirit-filled church where he met his future wife, Debi.

Because Guy made a decision to walk into church and cry out to God, many lives have been changed. Guy and Debi went to Bible school together in Tulsa, Oklahoma. They graduated and pioneered a successful church on the West Coast, which continues to this day—because of one cry.

The Lord is there for you, too—always. He never leaves you nor forsakes you (see Heb. 13:5). However, the Holy Spirit, the Lord's agent here on earth, is a gentleman. He will never override your will or force Himself into your life. And when the storms of life are raging, you can rise up and cry out to Him, the One who is your Rock, your sure anchor of hope in what appears to be a hopeless situation. You don't have to surrender to adversity, roll over, and play dead. Instead, you can look to Him and take authority over the opposition that tries to boldly withstand you.

You have another choice: you can be passive about the whole situation. Either way, there is no standing still in the spirit; you are either going forward or backward. Neutral is an untenable position. Being wishy-washy is detrimental. Even the Lord says in Revelation 3:16, *"Because you are lukewarm, and neither cold nor hot, I will spew you out of My mouth!"*

The enemy would rejoice if you just gave into the circumstances. But you have a wonderful God who wants the best for you. All He requires you to do is stand up, cry out, and listen for His instructions. When you give Him all the glory, He will win the battle for you. It does not matter how many are coming against you and how few are on your side to fight the hoard.

"Do not be afraid nor dismayed because of this great multitude, for the battle is not yours, but God's" (2 Chron. 20:15 NKJV).

During adversity, if you will look straight ahead like a horse wearing blinders, it will be as though His face is all you see. When you are determined to be that focused you are not going to allow the battle raging around you to distract you. You will recognize your authority to open the heavens with a cry and bring the Lord on the scene in your situation. Still, the key to success is to make use of that authority.

When the situation seems totally impossible in the natural and beyond any human means of help, it is time to shout to the only One who can—and will—help you. But remember three things when you cry to Him: always keep yourself in the love of God; walk in forgiveness; and keep winning souls. If you have unsaved loved ones for whom you are crying out, bear this promise in mind: *"He will even deliver one* [for whom you intercede] *who is not innocent; yes, he will be delivered through the purity of your hands"* (Job 22:30 NKJV).

Make sure you judge yourself and repent of anything that misses the mark before you cry out to God. He will honor the fact that you humbled yourself. He promises to exalt you in due time because of your humility! (See First Peter 5:6.) Dying to yourself in this way makes all the difference because, when you are humble, you open yourself up to God's perfect will.

Being open to God is the true meaning of humility. When you are full of pride, you close yourself off to Him and think your way is the only way. This is the way of our world; the focus is on self. God's way centers our focus on Him: *"Who may ascend into the hill of the Lord? Or, who may stand in His holy place? He who has clean hands and a pure heart…"* (Ps. 24:3-4 NKJV).

A pure heart keeps God at the center. When you focus on His righteousness and holiness, the things of this world grow strangely dim, including your own desires and plans for your life. According to Finis Jennings Dake, the holy place referred to in Psalms 24:3 "is the capital building of Christ" and the heavenly city referred to in Hebrews 12:22:[3]

> But ye are come unto mount Sion, and unto the city of the living God, the heavenly Jerusalem, and to an innumerable company of angels.

There are hosts of angels at your beck and call, but they can only act in accordance with His word. When you speak and act on that Word, they can move heaven and earth on your behalf. Just make sure you are not talking out of both sides of your mouth. You can't be like the man with cancer who speaks the Word every time the pastor comes to call on him and then goes to the kitchen table to prepare his funeral arrangements after the pastor leaves. A double-minded man receives nothing from the Lord.

A BROTHER CRIES OUT FOR HIS SISTER

While growing up in Memphis, Tennessee, my sister Janice and I would fish along the Mississippi River from a small boat. I would steer along the riverbanks so we could troll there. Meanwhile, Janice, who had an Annie Oakley-style scrapping spirit, would spot water moccasins hanging from the trees and pick them off with her shotgun.

A problem occurred on one of these adventures when a live water moccasin dropped into the boat! We jumped on it, stomped its head, and nearly capsized the boat.

Janice and I were always close, having shared many fun times growing up in the South. What we didn't share was an understanding of Jesus. The only thing we had ever heard about Him were the song lyrics, "Jesus loves me this I know, for the Bible tells me so."

Although we had good parents who cared for us, we never went to church or read the Bible. Unfortunately, our mother and father argued a lot and ended up getting a divorce. When I was 12 and Janice was 17, we moved to Las Vegas and continued to be the best of friends. She eventually became the top showgirl at the Tropicana Hotel on the Las Vegas Strip. I, on the other hand, had an encounter with God, was born again, and began preaching on the streets of Las Vegas. I eventually found my way into church.

Jan's life seemed glitzy and glamorous in those days. In reality, she was using methamphetamine and the drug was taking her downhill fast. She stood 5' 10" tall and lost so much weight that her ribs stuck out.

Emaciated showgirls are not good show business, so the Tropicana bumped Jan from her chorus line. She did even more drugs at that point and deteriorated quickly. Doctors committed her to a mental hospital and offered little hope for her survival, saying the drugs had destroyed her brain cells.

But God had other plans; He put a cry in my heart for her life. I was working as a janitor at a little church in North Las Vegas at the time and living there as well. I would fast and pray for days on end, asking the Lord for Jan to experience the same resurrection power that had changed me from a drug-peddling hippie to an on-fire evangelist.

Finally, my prayers were answered. Desperate to find God, my sister came calling at that little church. I will never forget the way she looked; she was practically on her hands and knees. This was my sister—the former showgirl who always had the best-looking men in the business at her beck and call; the one who had wined and dined with A-list celebrities.

For a down-home girl like Jan, the high life was not what it was cracked up to be. I remember hearing about one experience at a formal dinner with designer Oscar De La Renta. Jan unwittingly revealed her homespun heritage when she mistook a finger bowl for a bowl of soup, put it up to her lips in front of the whole crowd, and drank it down. We laughed over that story for years.

But when the decrepit drug addict of a showgirl stood at the door of the church that day, she looked straight into my eyes and said, "Do you think God can help me?" Skinny and forlorn, a far cry from her former glamorous self, Janice Hudson accepted Jesus Christ right there in that little North Las Vegas church.

Five years later, her life had totally turned around. Jan devoured the Word and attended church every time the doors opened. She had become an avid teacher and was eventually asked to be the Associate Pastor of that church. When Jan preached, she had a way of making Old Testament stories seem like they were part of your life. They sounded like modern stories you would read in *People Magazine*, but with a God ending.

Jan had a deep reverence for the Lord and a hunger to see the miraculous. My heart had cried out for God's mercy for my sister and she received a miracle in her life. That's how a cry works: if you follow God's divine flow of love, you will see people set free and blessed every time. You don't have to manufacture the cry. You will sense God's compassion welling up on the inside, compelling you to do something for someone else.

How does this happen? Just stay full of love and seek Him. Stay full of the Holy Ghost. Go about your business until you sense His prompting. You will learn to recognize when He has placed a certain person on your heart and when it is time to act. Do not hesitate! Pick up the phone, send them an email or text message, or visit them in person if that is possible. Just do whatever the Lord is directing you to do.

John Osteen, the father of Pastor Joel Osteen of Houston, Texas, used to practice this all the time. He said:

When the Lord moves on me in this way, flood-
ing in my heart with His supernatural love for an
individual, I pick up the telephone and dial their
number. I say, "Well, brother, I don't know what
your need is (unless God has revealed it to me),
but God has impressed me that He is going to
bless you today and that His love is flowing out
toward you. Whatever you have need of, you are
going to get it because God's love is shining on
your heart. God guided me today to minister to
you in the name of the Lord Jesus." Many times
these people have broken into tears and have said,
"Oh, you will never know the burden I've been
under!" But God knew.[4]

Jan encouraged some people at church to go for more of
God and attend Bible school. She knew there was more of God
for herself and the family she had built along the way, too. She
would pour over the Word, plumb its depths, and devour old
sermons by people like John G. Lake. Lake was an insurance-
agent-turned-minister who had a profound healing anointing on
his life. Lake had such remarkable results that, sometime around
1910, he was arrested in Spokane, Washington, for healing people
without a license.

Lake had seen more than 100,000 people healed in that one
city alone. This inspired Jan. She, her husband Phil, and small
daughter Jennifer decided to move to the Philippines to minister
healing in the slums of Angelus City. For two years, she saw
blind eyes open, limbs grow out, and people miraculously healed
of a variety of ailments. It would prove to be the highlight of
Jan's life.

However, in a tragic turn of events, Jan contracted breast
cancer while overseas. She did not get home in time to arrest its

spread and ended up going home to Heaven early. Still, Jan went a long way to fulfilling the call of God on her life.

Jan's fruitfulness was possible because one person stood in the gap with a cry for her salvation. That is exactly what it is going to take for you and your family too—a passionate cry beyond the norm, a fervent plea for help from the soul to the King of kings and Lord of lords. He is the One who is ready and able to answer your prayers.

A CRY WITH AN UNWELCOME ANSWER

Years ago several churches were holding a conference at a downtown Las Vegas, Nevada hotel-casino. Several well-known preachers were speaking; evangelist Benny Hinn was one of them. A gambler from the casino ran up to Hinn and challenged him saying, "I don't believe in God."

Hinn, walking up the stairs to the main conference room, quickly spun around to the man and replied, "Why, sir, your name is written in the Bible."

Curious, irritated, and indignant by this time, the unbeliever queried, "What are you talking about?"

Hinn calmly answered, "Psalms 53:1 says, *'The fool has said in his heart, "There is no God"'*" (NKJV).

That man's cry may not have gotten him the answer he wanted to hear, but the truth will set you free. What is a fool, anyway, except someone who knows better than to do what he is doing? The Hebrew word for fool, *nabal*, means "stupid, wicked, vile, impious."[5] Fools have a variety of characteristics: they deny the existence of God, live corrupt lives, do abominable works, ignore and fail to seek God, and lack understanding. Psalms 14:3 says: *"They are all gone aside, they are all together become filthy: there is none that doeth good, no, not one."*

Fools live in ignorance of God, and often destroy God's people. They are not likely to pray and often oppress the poor. In First Samuel 25:2-38, we read of just such a man. His name was *Nabal* and he lived up to his name by behaving foolishly. Nabal was a very wealthy and evil Judahite who mocked King David when David asked for food for his men. David pointed out that he and his army had protected the lives of Nabal's shepherds in the wilderness. Nabal was ungrateful and unimpressed. He didn't think he owed David anything, saying in effect, "Who is this guy anyway? I can't make provision for everyone who comes along."

David was the king of Israel at the time and was angered by Nabal's insulting remarks. David planned to kill Nabal and destroy all that he had. One of Nabal's servants told Nabal's wife, Abigail, what had transpired. Abigail quickly and secretly made provision to be generous to David's army without Nabal finding out.

Fortunately, Nabal's household was spared and Abigail made an impression on David because of her humility and graciousness. Nabal died shortly afterward and David made Abigail one of his favorite wives.

What saved Nabal from David's wrath was Abigail's willingness to cry out for mercy. Still, Nabal died within days of his defiance toward David.

> *Fools because of their transgression, and because of their iniquities, are afflicted. Their soul abhorreth all manner of meat; and they draw near unto the gates of death. Then they cry unto the Lord in their trouble, and He saveth them out of their distresses* (Psalms 107:17-19).

Those who don't cry out to God find themselves up against

a brick wall in life. Fools like Nabal depend on their own wisdom and refuse to listen to the Lord. Proverbs 29:1 warns that those who have hardened hearts and are stiff-necked will "... *be destroyed—without remedy.*"

God delivers us from the hard places when we cry out to Him and yield to His direction. This may involve a degree of discipline. It is never pleasant to undergo discipline, but those who yield to it and obey its correction become giants in the area of character.

> *Now no chastening seems to be joyful for the present, but painful; nevertheless, afterward it yields the peaceable fruit of righteousness to those who have been trained by it* (Hebrews 12:11 NKJV).

At times you may be so overwhelmed by circumstances that you become boxed into a corner. Your mind doesn't understand what needs to be done, but your spirit yearns to connect with Him. That is what is so remarkable about praying in tongues, your heavenly prayer language. It is your spirit praying to the Spirit of God and the devil cannot understand what you say. You start to make connection with Him, without even saying anything in English.

Not only that but, when you pray in the Spirit, you are praying out the plan for your life. First Corinthians 14:2 says you are praying "mysteries." "A mystery is an insight into some present-day Christian experience or future expectation not unveiled."[6]

When you yield to a spirit of prayer, you are making a divine connection with God. This connection is not intellectual, but spiritual. Often, when we pray for people to receive the Baptism in the Holy Spirit, they try to "figure out" how to speak in tongues. However, the Bible says when you pray in tongues, your mind is unfruitful; it is your spirit that prays! Your spirit communicates with God, who is the Father of all spirits.

A CRY FOR HELP

We must be set free in order to help those who are at the place where we once were. It's that way with Jesus; He understands our needs because He was *"...in all points tempted like as we are..."* (Heb. 4:15). Jesus understands the adversity we face because He has experienced it.

It is important for us to learn from the way Jesus handled His greatest challenge, the cross. Where did Jesus get the strength to endure it? Scripture tells us that He cried out to the Father: He *"...offered up prayers and supplications with strong crying and tears unto Him that was able to save Him from death..."* (Heb. 5:7).

Jesus was also aware that angelic assistance was available, as described in Hebrews 1:14: *"Are they not all ministering spirits, sent forth to minister for them who shall be heirs of salvation?"* Just when we feel as though we are about to lose it, we cry out and the angels come in and save us.

I have experienced the ministry of angels. One sunny afternoon I was driving the freeway along the California coast with my family. We had just spent a wonderful day fellowshiping with friends and were starting the two-hour ride back to our house. The trip was going smoothly; there seemed to be no problems. We were looking forward to getting home before dark. Our older, but well-maintained, BMW sedan was sailing down the fast lane; my wife, Mary, was in the passenger seat and my seven-year-old son was asleep in the back.

God has blessed me with eagle eyes. He shows me clearly and sharply what is ahead of me. All of a sudden, a truck with a fifth-wheel trailer passed us in the right lane. We noticed its back right wheel was wobbling, but thought nothing more of it than to catch up with the driver and let him know he needed to pull over and fix it.

All of a sudden, the wheel spun off the axle, went airborne and started coming right at our windshield! With a split second to spare, Mary screamed "Jesus!" It was obvious He was the only One who could save us from sudden destruction at that moment.

In a flash, the tire that had been whirling toward us like a giant rubber and steel platter dropped about a foot right in front of our eyes. It realigned itself right under the engine, as if a giant hand had pushed it out of harm's way. The airborne tire gently lifted the vehicle up onto the center divider of the highway. After landing with a slight thump, we sat there in shock and examined ourselves for injuries.

Although my back was a little out of joint, we were virtually unscathed. However, our car was totaled and the four-wheel trailer tire was jammed up under our engine.

We knew only an angel of the Lord could have intervened so quickly to save us from certain death. No doubt he was responsible for pushing that tire under the engine instead of through the windshield. Otherwise, it would have smashed right into our faces. Needless to say, after a short stop at the hospital to examine our injuries, which were very slight, we praised and blessed God all the way home.

What we experienced that day was a test; but out of it came a testimony. There are times when you have to go through a situation to find out whether you really believe the Word on which you are standing. You can't always avoid tests; but know this: every time you get the victory out of a trial, you reach a new level spiritually, a higher place in His glory. Trials may threaten to take you down and discourage you, but when you take God at His Word and cry out to Him, He is right there to rescue you. Whatever the trial, we know that *"if God be for us, who can be against us?"* (Rom. 8:31).

Trials aren't the only time we need to be alert. So often, we need to stand strong and get the victory in the hard times through our persistence. However people can lose their focus—and the victory—when everything is going smoothly, because they get complacent and lose their zeal.

Whatever the season you are in, it is vital to renew your mind daily in order to shore yourself up against the enemy's attacks. When your mind is renewed, you will refute his insinuations that you have lost the victory. You will use your voice to decree, declare, and cry out the truth of God's Word with your own breath.

There are many ways to renew your mind to His Word. When you hear a message preached in person, listen to a Word-filled CD, or watch a sermon on DVD, your mind is renewed. But receiving the Word is only half the story. For the Word to become effective in your life there must be some output, too.

The process can be compared to that of a recording device. Your recorder has an input; the data goes in and is saved. But what good is saving the sound if you can't play it back? God is not interested in religious rituals; religion stinks in the nostrils of God. What He wants is a relationship with you. He doesn't just want you to store up His Word; He wants to see His Word working in and through you.

God is purposeful and specific, not aimless and vague. When He prompted the writing of the book of Numbers, He gave great attention to detail. Likewise, when we turn on the output by speaking His Word, we must follow His lead and be accurate and specific.

Lawyers borrow this principle when arguing a legal case. They depend upon legal precedent (the exact wording, circumstances, and decisions from past cases) in order to present and win their arguments.

To experience victory in life, you stand on God's written

Word *and* on any personal word God has quickened to your heart. You will have to declare His Word out of your own mouth to make it effective and you will need to do it on a regular basis.

When you turn on the "output," you are announcing to Heaven, hell, and the whole earth that the same Word of God that created the world in the beginning will recreate your world and circumstances today.

DAVID CRIED AT HIS MIDNIGHT HOUR

David was a man whose confidence was placed wholly in God and His Word. When King Saul and his army hunted down David and swooped in for the kill, David trusted God and escaped their wrath. Psalms chapter 18 records David's praises to the Lord for this mighty victory over a seemingly insurmountable enemy.

At the core of the conflict was Saul's fear of David. Although David was not yet crowned king, he already had the kingly anointing on his life, as confirmed by the prophet, Samuel (see 1 Sam. 16:13).

Saul's days as king were numbered. He had disappointed the Lord at the battle of Amalek by not fully obeying the Lord's instructions. As a result, Saul lost the anointing that had been on his life.

God had told Saul to utterly destroy the Amalakites' town and everyone and everything in it. However, Saul destroyed only the common people and those items that were of little value. He spared the life of the Amalekite king and kept the Amalekites' valuables for himself. (See First Samuel 15:5-9.)

God's favor had now fallen upon David, His chosen replacement for Saul. Because God's hand was on David's life, Saul would not be able to destroy him, no matter how hard he tried.

Still, in the midst of the struggle, David's situation looked dire. The Book of Psalms records David's thoughts through many of these ups and downs. We can see from David's thank offerings to the Lord just how profoundly God turned the circumstances around and delivered David, who said: *"I will call upon the Lord, who is worthy to be praised; so shall I be saved from my enemies"* (Ps. 18:3 NKJV).

This is how you get the victory! You must call upon Him. Yield to a cry and He will show you the path of life. He will rescue you when fear surrounds you. David freely admitted his fear, saying, *"The pangs of death surrounded me* [Saul and his whole army were out to kill me and scoured the land for any trace of me], *and the floods of ungodliness made me afraid"* (Ps. 18:4 NKJV).

Yet fear did not overcome David. You might have a lot of negative thoughts attacking your mind, but you don't have to let them build a nest in your hair. There is a difference between having a thought and acting on what you think. The first action that follows a thought is the one you take with your tongue—it is what you say. What you say reveals whether you are acting on fear or acting in faith. You define what you believe first of all with your words.

David freely shared the secret to winning his battle with Saul:

> *In my distress I called upon the Lord, and cried out to my God; He heard my voice from His temple, and my cry came before Him, even to His ears* (Psalms 18:6 NKJV).

First of all, David recognized that there was no way he could succeed on his own. Crying out to God is what brought him the results he desired.

It is a humbling thing to cry out to anyone. When you cry out to God, you are saying, "Lord, I have tried every way I know, to no avail. Now Father, I open myself up to Your plan to fix this situation."

Pride is the opposite response. It literally closes you off to God's plan for your life by saying, "I can do this by myself. I know more than God. I can fix this." Pride emphasizes the big "I" instead of the Almighty One. Then, when you finally fall flat on your face or come to a screeching halt in life, you realize that you have shut the door to the only One who can help you.

When you cry out to the Lord, you are laying all your cards on the table and admitting your situation is no longer something you can control. Psalms 18:6 tells us that God heard David's cry! That means God hears *your* cry, because He is no respecter of persons.

This is not the time for rote prayers that get no answers. This is the time to cry for whatever the Lord is laying on your heart. Pouring out your heart like water before the Lord is the kind of prayer that gets the job done. We have been too religious, too lackluster, and even too legalistic on how, what, and when to pray. Now is the time to put a stop to the enemy's inroads with our cries, our heart, and our passion. This is a kairos moment, an era full of grace. We must be full of holy boldness and enter in where angels fear to tread.

In Psalms 18:7, the Lord begins to answer David's cry:

> *Then the earth shook and trembled; the foundations of the hills also quaked and were shaken, Because He was angry* (NKJV).

You really get a sense of the fear of the Lord from this verse. An earthquake of undetermined magnitude rumbled and woke up everyone when the Lord was aroused by injustice.

David was being tracked down by Saul, who had a massive army hunting him and his few armor bearers. It was an impossible, unfair situation in the natural. David was totally outnumbered. But David was nimble and sure-footed; He was so confident of supernatural intervention, even Saul's massive army could not find him.

David evaded his pursuers so well that he was able to cut off a piece of Saul's garment and prove the injustice of the situation (1 Sam. 24:4). David could have killed Saul at the same time and no one would have ever known he did it. But to prove his lack of malicious intent, David displayed the remnant of the robe and made his case to Saul:

> *Moreover, my father, see! Yes, see the corner of your robe in my hand! For in that I cut off the corner of your robe, and did not kill you, know and see that there is neither evil nor rebellion in my hand, and I have not sinned against you. Yet you hunt my life to take it.* (1 Samuel 24:11 NKJV).

David proved his loyalty to a man who wanted to take his life. David owed Saul nothing, but honored him because he was God's anointed. In spite of Saul's wicked intent toward David, the king-to-be kept his own heart pure. He served the one true God who does the impossible and reminds us that we cannot do it on our own.

Psalms 18:8 shows us that, not only did the earth shake when David cried out to God, but God got so mad that *"smoke went up from His nostrils, and devouring fire from His mouth; coals were also kindled by it"* (NKJV). No wonder the fear of the Lord was on the Jewish people! They saw God in all His magnificence and terror.

Do you know how hard it is to kindle a coal without firestarter? Have you ever tried starting a barbeque using charcoal briquettes that weren't saturated with kerosene? No! But God didn't need any natural help—He was so mad he just got the coals going with a blast of His nostrils.

Still, the display of God's righteous indignation was not complete. Consider Psalm 18:9-10:

> *He bowed the heavens also, and came down with darkness under His feet. And He rode upon a cherub, and flew; He flew upon the wings of the wind* (NKJV).

God wastes no time when He hears a cry from His people. Psalm 18:13-14 goes on to say:

> *The Lord thundered from heaven, and the Most High uttered His voice, hailstones and coals of fire. He sent out His arrows and scattered the foe, lightnings in abundance and He vanquished them* (NKJV).

When God hears your voice, He will take care of those who contend with you and He will do it with a magnificent display of power, if necessary. *"And He vanquished them."* God does the dirty work for you and He always finishes the job.

Verse 16 continues *"He sent from above, He took me; He drew me out of many waters"* (NKJV). Listen, God will even save you from drowning if you will cry out to Him.

Verse 17 says *"He delivered me from my strong enemy, from those who hated me, for they were too strong for me"* (NKJV). When Saul and the whole Israelite army were chasing down David and his few men, it looked like David was completely defeated. However, when God is on your side, a mighty host is fighting for you.

Your case may seem like an impossible situation with the

odds totally stacked against you. Your husband or wife may have already left you or even divorced you. You may have lost your house in a foreclosure or your business may have dried up. You may have a terminal disease; the doctors may be saying there is no hope for you. Perhaps you are a pastor and half of the congregation has walked out on you. Regardless of what you are facing, the moment you decide to cry out to Him is the moment when the situation will start to turn around.

God can do anything; the real question is whether we are willing to humble ourselves under His mighty hand and yield to His leadings. He will exalt us in due time when we submit ourselves to His guidance. Humility is the key.

But what is humility? Let's start with what humility is not: Being humble does not mean beating yourself up mentally, physically, or any other way. Nor does being humble mean that you must wear a hair shirt like John the Baptist wore.

The word *humility* describes an attitude of openness to the will of God for your life. When you are full of pride, you put yourself, your will, and your plans first. You shut the door to the Lord. That is what Lucifer did: *"...O Lucifer, son of the morning!... Thou hast said in thine heart, I will ascend into heaven, I will exalt my throne above the stars of God..."* (Isa. 14:12-13). But did Lucifer ever have a big fall coming! *"Yet thou shalt be brought down to hell, to the sides of the pit"* (Isa. 14:15). Mind you, the enemy knows his time is short and that's why he is launching such vicious attacks. That is why we must advance with even more aggressive weapons of our warfare.

Now David had a clear view of the battle lines during his trial; he knew who was with him and who was against him. He said in Psalm 18:18, "[my enemies] *confronted me in the day of my calamity, but the Lord was my support"* (NKJV).

You, too, will have battles during which your enemies will confront you, but when you cry out and cast the care of the fight on God, He will be there to undergird you. He will never let you down. He will even celebrate you. *"He also brought me out into a broad place; He delivered me because He delighted in me"* (Psalm 18:19 NKJV).

SUMMARY

1. There is a cry in God's heart and He wants it to become the cry of yours.

2. In the midst of a crisis, do what you can do and God will do the rest.

3. Trust God. No matter how insurmountable the odds, you can rest in God's goodness.

4. Recognize your authority to open the heavens with a cry and bring the Lord into every situation.

5. Be alert when times are difficult; be just as alert when everything seems to be going well.

CHAPTER TWO

IT'S TIME
TO CRY

And at midnight there was a cry made, Behold,
the bridegroom cometh... (Matthew 25:6).

There is a kairos moment when you must cry. This cry is a heartfelt sound that builds and builds until the moment for its release arrives.

Matthew 25:6 is a great example of a coming kairos moment. God is going to put such a passionate cry on the inside of His people that when we go into His chambers, all we're going to do is stand there and weep before Him.

God wants to hear your heart. We can gain a lot of knowledge, we can become very intelligent, we can learn all the Scriptures; but there is a greater realm, a greater depth of prayer when your heart speaks directly and intimately to Him.

He is going to put a cry in your heart so you can begin to hear Him and minister effectively. We see people crying all the time in airports. God places great value on their tears. We have His compassion, so we want to go over and minister to hurting people. Most of the time we do. God is preparing us to become more sensitive—to Him and to others.

This is important, because, to usher in the soon-coming King of kings and Lord of lords, there must be a cry from the hearts of men and women. I believe Jesus has not come back yet because there is no such cry from the Church. But the exciting thing is that He is putting this cry inside us.

Sometimes you hit an impasse in your Christian life when nothing is happening and everything seems stagnant. That is the time when nothing but a cry piercing the heavens will break the stalemate.

You might be driving along the freeway in your car when, suddenly, this cry erupts out of your innermost being. It is a desire to reconnect with God and get back to the place where you left off with Him.

You do not have to get in touch with God because it is your "religious duty." When you reach out to Him in passionate prayer, it opens a pathway to sharing intimate times of fellowship with your heavenly Father. This fellowship will bring much peace into your life.

Sometimes we reach an impasse when we do not see what God is doing with our prayers; we get discouraged and lose heart. But make no mistake; if you prayed, then something is happening, even if it isn't obvious to your natural mind.

For a tree to grow large, the roots have to go down deep. It takes time to develop a strong root system and we sometimes grow impatient with the process. It is easy to give up when you don't see any manifestations. That is the time to cry out to Him. When you do, the Holy Spirit may show you spiritual roadblocks that have been hindering you. He'll help you to see clearly what you are dealing with. He may reveal hindrances such as unforgiveness and selfishness. This is the point at which some people stop praying. They just don't believe the problem is their fault, or they don't want to venture into these "dark closets" in their lives.

It is like the drawer that you haven't cleaned out in five years. Everything imaginable is stuffed in there. You know that sorting it all out is going to create a big mess, so you avoid dealing with it. Spiritually speaking, however, you can't move on to the next phase God has planned for your life until you sort out the current phase.

There are other options: If you don't mind staying stuck where you are, you can do nothing and learn to live with the mess. Another approach is that of believers in New Age philosophy; they think God is a magician who will automatically change everything around them.

However, these options are dead ends. As the Lord lovingly points out: when we abide in Him and He abides in us, *then* we can ask what we will and it *shall* be done unto us (see John 15:7). It is when we make that decision to abide in Him that we are changed from glory to glory.

Christianity is not a spectator religion; it is a vibrant, participatory relationship with the living God and His Son, Jesus, who ever lives to make intercession for us (see Heb. 7:25). You are going to have to participate by taking authority over emotions such as discouragement, defeat, and depression—emotions which may have ruled your life for a long time.

You counter-attack these emotions with God's Word. The Word that is embedded in your mind is the only thing that can overrule those emotions. If you will maintain your faith and be persistent in fervent prayer, you will make it through any emotional impasse. The Holy Spirit will show you how ugly these works of the flesh are and He will give you the strength to deal with them effectively.

With the help of the Holy Spirit, you will have the strength to truly repent, mortify your flesh, and enjoy total victory in your mind and freedom in your heart. After you break through a barrier of this kind, God will be better able to use you. That is part of the hope of being transformed by Him—it is what makes us more apt to allow the Holy Spirit to expose our selfishness, pride, and anger sooner rather than later.

Surely, having your sin dealt with now is better than waiting until you become the pastor of a 10,000-member church. If your emotions are not dealt with, you might lash out at the congregation when the associate pastor (whom you have diligently and lovingly mentored for seven years) decides to split your church and take 100 people down the road to start another work.

Many times the Holy Spirit will give you signs along the way to warn that problems like this are about to surface, just as He gives prophecies to foretell things that are about to be fulfilled.

The Holy Spirit certainly gave Israel ample notice of the coming of the Messiah. There were hundreds of years between the Lord's deliverance of Israel and the arrival of Jesus. But the Lord put signposts along Israel's path; these divine directives, signs, and wonders announced that the Messiah was on His way. God's promises about Him were clear.

Prophets such as Ezekiel gave Israel words of hope such as this:

> *A new heart also will I give you, and a new spirit will I put within you: and I will take away the stony heart out of your flesh, and I will give you*

an heart of flesh. And I will put My Spirit within you, and cause you to walk in My statutes, and ye shall keep My judgments and do them (Ezekiel 36:26-27).

If you will pay attention, He will make sure you don't miss His signs. However, if you choose to ignore them, you risk getting totally sidetracked and off the path for your life.

A CLEAR PATH

In these last days God is making His path so evident that it is almost hard to miss it. But if you do miss it, just cry out to Him for further direction. In John Bunyan's 17th-century classic, *The Pilgrim's Progress*, even the devout Pilgrim got off the track for a period of time. But through the help of a person used by the Holy Spirit, he regained his footing and got back on the path.

I don't know how the Lord talks to you, but sometimes He gives me a Scripture paragraph or chapter or even a sign on the side of the road. He can speak to you through the Word or He can speak to you through people. He knows how to get your attention. He will speak to you differently from the way He speaks to me. If you are sensitive to His leadings, there are many ways God can communicate with you.

One day I was driving down the road near my house, heading for the local dry cleaners. We live in a bedroom community of Los Angeles and San Diego, California. It has had explosive growth in recent years, with housing developments mushrooming throughout the large valley.

As I was driving, a brand-new development caught my eye. It had over 100 new homes for sale. There was a big white fence around these beautiful $400,000 to $500,000 units. A huge vinyl sign on the fence boldly announced "Final Phase Has Been Released." When I saw that sign, it was as though the words jumped off of it, flew inside my car, and stood up right in front of me. The Lord spoke to my heart and said, "Son, tell them the final phase has been released on this earth."

You and I are living in the final phase of history as we know it. We are living in the days about which Isaiah, Jeremiah, and Daniel prophesied. If we all understood the days we are part of, many of our problems would disappear. The only problem pastors would face would be overwhelming church growth.

If we really understood the times, we would get it together. We would make some adjustments and live right. We would not have to be rescued or prayed for. We would not beg God to get us out of one predicament only to find ourselves in another one.

Do you know the day and the hour you are living in? Can you see the stop sign God is illuminating right in front of us? In other times and seasons, the cry for change may not have been so desperate or passionate. But now we have reached a period in history where the needs and conflicts in people's lives and society are so much more acute that a cry is the only remedy. Other solutions may have worked in the past, but only a cry will do now.

BECOME PASSIONATE

It is time for passion in your Christian walk as never before. Your DNA is unique. If you have been born again, you are full of the fire of God; but it may be buried under a mask of religion, hurts, or disappointments.

Passion burns deep within you and sometimes you just have to let it out. Many people think Christians are strange when they raise their hands and give praise to a God whom they believe is alive. Yet, non-believers don't think twice about standing in line all night for the best seat in the football stadium. They don't think it's strange to paint their faces like Native American warriors or hoop and holler for their favorite team while standing for hours in the frigid cold.

What distinguishes the passionate worshiper from the fervent fan is the matter of spirit and flesh. Although both are likely to raise their hands high in the air and show emotion, one (the God-worshiper) is responding in the Spirit while the other (the sports fanatic) is responding in the flesh.

Throughout the centuries, the people of God have responded to him in the Spirit. This has produced unusual occurrences, from the world's perspective. The Baptism of the Holy Ghost was birthed in fire—"cloven tongues" of fire according to Acts 2:2.

Elijah called down fire and it consumed waterlogged wood and sacrifices, a virtual physical impossibility (see 1 Kings 18:38). Three Hebrew children were thrown into the fierce flames of a fiery furnace, yet they didn't burn. Instead, they were joined in the fire by a fourth person—a man who looked like the Son of God! (See Daniel 3:25.)

The prophet Amos was a mere shepherd on the hills of Israel when the Spirit of God gave him a vision of the earthquake the Lord would bring to the land (see Amos 1:1). Like John the Baptist, Amos cried out to prepare the people. He stressed the importance of unity during the upcoming calamity asking: *"Can two walk together, except they be agreed?"* (Amos 3:3). He also reminded the people to listen to their prophets instead of the local authorities:

> *Surely the Lord God will do nothing, but he revealeth His secret unto His servants the prophets. The lion hath roared, who will not fear? the Lord God hath spoken, who can but prophesy?* (Amos 3:7-8).

In other words, God will give you signposts along the way, whether they are unusual experiences that stand out or words from seasoned prophets. Don't ignore these prophetic promptings when they show up. They are hints from the Holy Ghost about what He is about to do in your life.

Likewise, when God's cry roars through your spirit prompting you to prophesy, don't hold back. Lives will be changed and destinies altered when you allow Him to use you as the vessel through which He speaks. Don't resist God's plan as some did in Amos' day. God pointed out the results of their resistance to Him saying, *"I have overthrown some of you, as God overthrew Sodom and Gomorrah, and ye were as a firebrand plucked out of the burning: yet have ye not returned unto Me"* (Amos 4:11).

Then the Lord told Amos His people would have to walk according to the pattern the Lord set.

> *Thus He shewed me: and, behold, the Lord stood upon a wall made by a plumbline, with a plumbline in His hand. And the Lord said unto me, Amos, what seest thou? And I said, a plumbline. Then said the Lord, Behold, I will set a plumbline in the midst of My people Israel: I will not again pass by them any more* (Amos 7:7-8).

Your mind is strong and God wants to create new thought patterns to replace your old ideas. Those who have graduated from high school have completed at least 12 years of educating their minds. Most of us live under the rule of a mind trained by secular education, that is, until we decide to accept salvation and replace our intellectual thinking with the mind of Christ.

When we start reading our Bibles, life really starts to change because we learn to think like God. Even so, to the degree that the mind is unrenewed it will "reason" with you the way satan reasoned with Eve in The Garden when he asked, *"Hath God [really] said...?"* (Genesis 3:1).

The enemy was trying to get Eve to compromise by believing that eating the apple was not such a big deal; He will speak to you the same way. He will reason with you through an unrenewed mind and suggest to you that smoking...drinking...or having an affair is not such a big deal. The enemy uses the same bag of tricks today that he did then.

To protect yourself from his tactics, change your perspective; see if what he is telling you lines up with God's Word. Satan wanted Adam and Eve to give up on God; he wants you to do the same. When you give in to satan and disobey what God has told you, you end up going a giant step backward when you could have gone two steps forward. This is a big deal to God, because you can lose everything you have gained.

Adam and Eve sure did. They lost their place in The Garden of Eden, a life so perfect all they really had to do was pick the fruit off the trees and worship and fellowship with the Lord daily. This was God's ideal pattern—to begin the human race with two people formed in His image, people with whom He could be in continuous relationship.

All Adam and Eve had to do was obey God. Instead, Eve decided to eat from the only tree God said was off limits. For that, she and Adam lost everything. Eating a single apple does not seem like a big deal, but partaking of it had huge consequences for their lives and the whole human race.

Your choices today can affect generations to come. When Adam and Eve were ushered out of The Garden, it seemed as though all hope for mankind was lost. Thankfully, God came forth with a new plan in Genesis 3:15 saying: *"I will put enmity between thee and the woman, and between thy seed and her seed; it shall bruise thy head, and thou shalt bruise his heel."*

God flat out prophesied to the deceiving serpent that Jesus would be the price the Lord would pay to restore His relationship with man. The fact remains: when you hear a word from God or read a Scripture that resonates with your spirit, grab hold of it without hesitation. When God instructs you, do what He says.

Under the New Testament we live under new and better promises that make us free. You could say we have everything. Yet, not everything that is available to us is expedient for us.

When Adam and Eve were cast out of The Garden, life became a whole lot more difficult. They were forced to live by the sweat of their brow. One of their children, Cain, actually killed their other child, Abel. A curse remained on mankind until Jesus came and died for us and broke that curse on the cross.

All the Lord requires of us is to live by the plumbline of His Word. He doesn't just want to visit us, He wants to live with us throughout our lives. His heart is to be right in the middle of our lives, leading and guiding us into all truth. We receive that guidance by fellowshiping with Him in the Word and in prayer on a daily basis. It is not like we have to struggle to do that, we just flow with it.

An apple tree does not struggle to produce an apple. The fruit just shows up as the result of the tree being planted in the ground, nurtured, fertilized, and watered. The apple grows as an extension of daily abiding in the limb of that tree and partaking of all the nutrients that are poured into it. As you read the Word and allow His precepts to abide in your everyday life, your fruit will start to show up, too.

END-TIME SIGNS

The book of Amos ends with these comforting prophecies:

Behold, the days come, saith the Lord, that the plowman shall overtake the reaper, and the treader of grapes him that soweth seed; and the mountains shall drop sweet wine, and all the hills shall melt. And I will bring again the captivity of My people of Israel, and they shall build the waste cities, and inhabit them; and they shall plant vineyards, and drink the wine thereof; they shall also make gardens, and eat the fruit of them. And I will plant them upon their land, and they shall no more be pulled up out of their land which I have given them, saith the Lord thy God (Amos 9:13-15).

In these end times events are going to happen quickly. Things that you have imagined happening over the course of decades or years will occur at a much more rapid clip—in months or weeks or even days.

Why? Because the time is truly short and Jesus is coming back soon. Just watch the nightly news. Compare it with Bible prophecy and figure it out. When these things start to happen, you must be the watchman on the wall, a seer ready to cry out a warning at the first sign of attack or opportunity.

Elijah was just such a watchman. He persisted in sending his servant out seven times to look for signs of rain. After so many unfruitful trips, that servant must have been wondering what his master was doing. But then it showed up, just when the servant was giving up hope! The servant announced, *"There ariseth a little cloud out of the sea, like a man's hand"* (1 Kings 18:44).

Our world is filled with signs, wonders, and prophetic indications of the Lord's soon return. They are manifested in the groanings of the earth as earthquakes, tsunamis, hurricanes, and tornadoes become more frequent and more violent.

Many people have experienced overwhelming circumstances in our day, trials that seem never-ending to the natural eye. Sometimes, the issues are much bigger than our ability, or anybody's ability, to manage.

Except for God! When you can't see any way out of your situation, you know it is time to cry out to God. King David knew this and said, *"I waited patiently for the Lord; and He inclined unto me, and heard my cry. He brought me also up out of an horrible pit, out of the miry clay, and set my feet upon a rock, and established my goings"* (Psalm 40:1-2).

Let's establish that a "horrible pit" is not a water well; it is a deep hole filled with mire and slime. The further you sink into the pit, the blacker and thicker the muck seems to get.

When you're in the pit, it feels as though you'll never get out of it. But God has a way of escape; you must believe that and not try to second-guess Him. Rest in His Word. Trust that if He said He hears your cry and has promised to bring you out of the situation, He will do it.

Trust His timing, also. Sometimes, our problems seem never-ending. In reality, they don't last forever; they last for a season. He will bring you *up and out* of whatever "horrible pit" you are in and His timing will be perfect.

Thank God that He is your Rock, your firm foundation. When you lose your footing in the slippery mire...when you can't seem to pull yourself out, He will place your feet upon the Rock and establish your steps.

Maybe you're not in the "horrible pit"; perhaps you are standing still in what seems to be a safe and secure place. You *still* need God. He will get you moving in the right direction. And, when every movement you make is ordered of the Lord, you will really make some headway in your life.

Psalm 40:3 says: *"He hath put a new song in my mouth, even praise unto our God: many shall see it, and fear, and shall trust in the Lord."* Not only does God rescue us from insurmountable odds, but He also cleans us up, establishes us, gets us moving again and gives us a fresh vision to sing about.

When He rescues you, your deliverance becomes a witness to everyone around you. You need to proclaim your testimony and tell others how the cry brought you through the test and into the testimony.

Testifying gives God the glory. The Lord is not silent about His delivering power. When He returns, it will not be a quiet event. We know, first of all, that *"the Lord Himself shall descend from heaven with a shout, with the voice of the archangel, and with the trump of God..."* (1 Thess. 4:16). A shout from God, an archangel's voice and God's trumpet—none of these are low, subtle sounds. This is radical warlike noise, piercing the skies as the Lord levels His final "checkmate" against the enemy.

Satan's game will finally be over for a season—at least for all true Christians on earth at that moment—and he knows it. That cry from God will raise the dead *"For the Lord Himself will come down from heaven with a **loud command**, with the voice of an archangel and with the trumpet call of God, and the dead in Christ will rise first. After that, we who are still alive and are left will be caught up together with them in the clouds to meet the Lord in the air. And so we will be with the Lord forever"* (1 Thess. 4:16-17 NIV, emphasis added)—all because of a cry.

Consider how the walls of Jericho came down with a shout! One shout of faith can break down all kinds of walls in your life. But when the Israelites surrounded Jericho, they did not do it haphazardly. The Lord gave them specific directions; they had this planned out. First of all, He told them the land belonged to them no matter what it looked like. *"And the Lord said to Joshua: 'See! I have given Jericho into your hand, its king and the mighty men of valor'"* (Josh. 6:2 NKJV).

Now, just because God shows you that something belongs to

you, and just because He puts His stamp of favor on it for you, it doesn't mean you won't have to fight to possess it in the natural. You *will* need to fight. There may be ruling spirits opposing you for the person, place, or thing God has promised. Regardless of how long these entities have dominated your promised "territory," they will not release it to you without a struggle.

That said, the sixth chapter of Joshua is an example of how God can change anything—and in just 24 hours' time. He instructed the Israelites to march around Jericho once a day for six days. Imagine how disconcerting that must have been for those who lived inside Jericho's walls. The army of Israelites circled Jericho the way a wolf circles its prey.

Imagine the torment, the noise of the army, the dust flying in the air. The scene reeked of impending doom for the inhabitants of Jericho. It would almost have been better for the Jerichoites to have the Israelites attack them on the first day. But no, the children of Israel had heard from their Master. They knew God was putting this city on the defense with fear and suspense before they could even start the actual battle.

That is exactly what you do when you confess the Word of God with authority over your situation: you encircle the situation the same way the Israelites encircled Jericho. From where you are, the problem may seem overwhelming (the walls of Jericho looked indestructible); but just keep reminding yourself that God is bigger than anything you could ever face.

When you open your mouth and declare and decree change into an impossible situation, the Lord fires up and backs up every breath you take. When the Lord gave Joshua and the children of Israel the order to shout down the walled city of Jericho, the walls were thick enough to run a chariot around. It was a situation where you could easily say, "Lord, You don't need my lungs to shout at this wall, you need a tornado to get this job done!"

But the same God who fed five thousand men (plus the

women and children who were with them) on five loaves and two fishes in Matthew 14 knew what He needed—it was the Israelites' instant faith in action:

> *And seven priests shall bear seven trumpets of rams' horns before the ark. But the seventh day you shall march around the city seven times, and the priests shall blow the trumpets. It shall come to pass, when they make a long blast with the ram's horn, and when you hear the sound of the trumpet, that all the people shall shout with a great shout;* **then** *the wall of the city will fall down flat...* (Joshua 6:4-5 NKJV, emphasis added).

Those walls didn't just fall down, but they fell down *flat*—flatter than pancakes! Excavations of the wall of Jericho show that the walls actually sank into the foundations when that unified shout joined the noise of the priests' trumpets and leveled that collection of giant boulders.

When the seventh day dawned, the inhabitants of Jericho were already in a state of fear; they had watched the Israelites encircle their city once a day for six days. Jericho's people were already intimidated, sensing that this would be a losing battle.

Israel demonstrated their preparedness, determination, and boldness. They instilled fear in the hearts of their opponents and the men of Jericho backed down.

That's what happens when you put on the full armor of God (see Eph. 6:13-17): your head is covered with the helmet of salvation; the breastplate of righteousness protects your chest; your feet are covered with the preparation of the Gospel of peace; the belt of truth is around your waist; and the sword of the Spirit is ready at your side. You are armed and dangerous. You know who you are in Christ and you rattle the devil's cage. Satan gets nervous when you know who you are in Christ, because he knows he is a defeated foe. He just doesn't want *you* to know it.

At the moment before victory was manifested, Joshua reminded the Israelites: *"Shout, for the Lord has given you the city!"* (Josh. 6:16 NKJV). It is so important to have a cry in battle. Many battles worldwide have started and ended with a cry. The most ferocious warlike cry can strike fear in the enemy's heart even before the actual fighting begins. And in Jericho's case that is exactly what happened. Except for Rahab the harlot who had hidden two Israelite spies (see Josh. 2), the place was utterly destroyed.

The enemy may have launched a vicious attack on you, but you can rout him with your voice; you can send him running with your cry to the Lord. The key is to keep moving and not stand still in terror. Don't be intimidated by the size of the problem or the insinuations that come against your mind. As you advance with a bold and determined shout, the enemy will retreat in panic.

It worked for Joshua against Jericho. It worked for David against Goliath. It worked for Jesus against satan on the Mount of Temptation.

It will work for you, too.

SUMMARY

1. God is going to put a cry in your heart so you can begin to hear Him and minister more effectively.

2. Christianity is not a spectator religion; it is a vibrant, participatory relationship with the living God and His Son, Jesus Christ.

3. Pay attention and God will make sure you don't miss the signposts He places along your path.

4. We have reached a period in history where the needs and conflicts faced by people and societies are so acute that a cry is the only remedy.

5. When you open your mouth to declare and decree change in an impossible situation, the Lord will fire up and back up every breath you take.

CHAPTER THREE

YOUR CRY
MATTERS

I am weary with my groaning; all night I make my bed swim; I drench my couch with my tears. My eye wastes away because of grief.... Depart from me, all you workers of iniquity; for the Lord has heard the voice of my weeping. The Lord has heard my supplication; the Lord will receive my prayer. Let all my enemies be ashamed and greatly troubled; let them turn back and be ashamed suddenly (Psalm 6:6-10 NKJV).

In this psalm, David describes his growing weariness with some type of affliction. David was accustomed to difficulty; early in his life, he had lived virtually in exile, hiding from Saul. Living in caves (even with his mighty men surrounding him) and eating whatever crossed their path must have become tiresome after a while.

Camping can be fun, but living in a tent and getting water from the river for a lifetime is another story. Winter can be harsh; the lack of plumbing can be challenging. Coming home to a clean bath after war is a treat to which most warriors would look forward.

During David's days on the run from Saul, he endured the situation. But he was also determined that being hunted by Saul's army throughout the hills of Judea would not last forever. David knew he was anointed to be king. Even though he had not attained the throne yet, the desire was already burning in David's heart. And although Saul was motivated by the jealousy that consumed him, it was no match for the power of God's hand on David.

When your enemies chase you down to destroy you, you have got to remember that you are not fighting against *"flesh and blood, but against principalities, against powers, against the rulers of the darkness of this world, against spiritual wickedness in high places"* (Eph. 6:12).

It may not seem like these spirits will ever give up, but the fact is that Jesus has already destroyed the works of the devil for you. Satan is under your feet. Jesus is there upholding you in the middle of the struggle. He has provided the spiritual armor you need to *"...be able to withstand in the evil day, and having done all, to stand"* (Eph. 6:13).

While you are standing, do not get stressed out. Instead, enter into His rest. Start to rejoice. God is serious when He says that *"the joy of the Lord is your strength"* (Neh. 8:10). Peace and joy demonstrate to the enemy that you have the upper hand. Your rest in the midst of turmoil shows that you are not moved by his machinations. You know God is going to win in the end.

It must have taken a lot of nerve and a lot of peace for David to quietly slice off a corner of Saul's garment without the great king realizing it. Then, for David to wave it at Saul and imply that Saul's men did a shoddy job of guarding him was risky. Yet, David knew that if he continued to walk in the anointing and in peace, the throne would eventually be his. Still, it was critical for him to make his supplication before the Lord and rest in Him in order to attain breakthrough. To prevail, David had to be persistent and not give up, in spite of the army that was chasing him around Israel.

David knew his God. He knew God *"had heard the voice of [his] weeping"* (Ps. 6:8). David's tears had a voice and that voice had come before the Lord. *"You number and record my wanderings; put my tears into Your bottle—are they not in Your book?"* (Ps. 56:8 AMP).

Collecting tears in a bottle was an ancient custom. Often, an offering of tears was left in the tomb or on the grave of a departed loved one. In Persian funerals the priest would collect tears onto cotton and squeeze them into a special bottle. Some Persians believed that when all other "medicines had failed, a drop of tears into the mouth of a dying man would revive him."[1]

Even before David witnessed Saul's destruction, he was sure that God had heard his cry. Therefore, he knew his enemies would be made ashamed and greatly troubled. David was confident that their lives would end suddenly. That is just what happened to Saul and his family in the midst of battle with the Philistines. Saul's kingdom was torn from him; he died in the heat of the battle without warning. (See First Samuel 31.)

David persevered through hard times. He kept doing the right things. Lack of follow-through can be a problem for Christians at times. They get so close to a breakthrough, then they quit praying because they see no results. God will give you a confirming word that the answer has come, but you cannot passively take it for granted. Doing so would be like climbing within ten yards of a mountaintop and retreating because you think you'll never see the summit.

The enemy and his minions clap their hands when Christians give up. Fortunately, we always have the Holy Spirit. He is our aide, comforter, and helper; He will get us back on track when we ask Him to.

Sometimes incredibly tragic things happen to people: babies and young children go to Heaven early; houses are foreclosed; spouses die before their time; tsunamis kill hundreds of thousands; earthquakes and hurricanes take the lives of many. When tragedy strikes, it can knock the wind out of you. But, all of a sudden, when the breath of the Holy Spirit blows through you again, the Lord re-ignites you in the Word.

For example, Jesus asked the man at the Pool of Bethesda, *"Wilt thou be made whole?"* (John 5:6)—in other words, "Are you going to stand up and fight this thing?"

Answered prayer in any situation is a matter of standing up on the inside first. The Lord was speaking to that man's spirit before He was speaking to his body. The man was shocked that anyone would say that to him. Imagine, of all people, Jesus our Healer asking such a question!

The man probably thought, "He'll just reach out and touch me and I'll be made whole." But the Lord needed the man's will to be in agreement with God's will. That man had been lying there for 38 years, waiting for an angel to stir the water at the right time. He was depending on another being to do it for him. But God doesn't want us leaning on others, not even famous preachers with a healing anointing. He wants us to take our healing for ourselves. That is the only way we are going to keep it.

The man at the Pool of Bethesda immediately reverted to excuse-making when the Answer stood right in front of him. He told Jesus he didn't have anyone to help him get into the water at the moment the angel showed up. But that was not what kept the man from being healed. After such a long period of time, this man had literally given up on the inside. Sickness and lack had worn him down.

But Jesus, ever full of compassion and mercy, saw this and continued to reach out to him. The man's final excuse was to say "...*But while I am coming, another steppeth down before me*" (John 5:7). The Lord ignored this comment. He did not even consider it worth answering. Instead, He immediately went to the heart of the matter, saying, *"Rise, take up thy bed, and walk"* (John 5:8). Jesus was saying, "Stand up on the inside. Do something you could not do before. Start moving."

You might be wallowing in a pool of self-pity over a seemingly insurmountable situation in your own life. Be encouraged by what Scripture says:

> *The Lord God is my Strength, my personal bravery, and my invincible army; He makes my feet like hinds' feet and will make me to walk [not to stand still in terror, but to walk] and make [spiritual] progress upon my high places [of trouble, suffering, or responsibility]!* (Habakkuk 3:19 AMP).

God's Word is empowering. When Jesus speaks to your heart and tells you to get going, know that He is saying it is your time to move. It is a kairos moment of favor on your life. If you allow the moment to slip by, you could be set back for years.

How often had Jesus passed by the pool and seen that man lying there? Who knows? But this was *the* moment—a split second where the lame man had a choice to make. He could choose to rise to the occasion or he could stay lame for years to come, hoping that Jesus would pass by again.

Who knows if Jesus would ever have been moved to call

out this man for healing again? No, the lame man had to act the moment Jesus called out to him. You also must act when the Lord calls you for a certain purpose in your life. When He speaks to you to arise out of your circumstances of sickness, poverty, or any kind of lack in your life, your response will determine whether you receive at that moment or not. Even when He is calling you out of one not-so-bad level of existence into a higher place of fellowship and intimacy with Him, you cannot afford to miss your moment.

The lame man's first response of "Sir, I have no one to put me into the water" got him nowhere. Just because you didn't get healed in a healing line in the past does not mean you won't get healed next time. It just means you need to keep going whenever you sense the anointing of the Lord is present to heal.

Fortunately Jesus, in His mercy, did not pass this man by just because he had a victim mentality. Jesus reached beyond the man's shortcomings. He does the same for us. When He speaks to us, He creates a bridge in the spirit realm for us to cross over. You can rely on the fact that He will not let you down if you continue to follow Him.

Do you remember when Jesus called Peter to walk on the water? Jesus told Peter to *"Come"* (Matt. 14:29); Peter obeyed and walked on the water! Peter didn't lose his footing until he looked at the circumstances. According to Matthew's Gospel: *"When* [Peter] *saw the wind boisterous, he was afraid; and beginning to sink, he cried, saying, Lord, save me"* (Matt. 14:30).

Peter became afraid and decided the wind and waves were bigger than God. Of course he started to sink! But the great part of the story is that Peter got back up again when the Lord grabbed his hand—and you can too! His hand of mercy is always extended to you. Just get moving and do whatever you can while you're in a tight place.

The first step is to use your voice and call out to Him. When you open your mouth with faith-filled words, you are taking action. It is movement; it is faith in action and that is what the Lord is looking for. You speak His Word and He watches over His Word to perform it. Just make sure yours is the right kind of action, relying on the only Source in the universe who can help you, and not on man or his solutions.

At the Pool of Bethesda, the Lord decided to demonstrate the truth of His healing power to a man who had wasted nearly a generation waiting in the wrong place. The man was not expecting a miracle, but he got one. Instead of looking to God, the man had looked to an angel, a mere messenger of God. (Angels cannot heal you; but they can point you in the direction of the Healer.) It was Jesus whom the man really needed.

You do not need to wait for your miracle; you need to act. You can sit, stand, or lie there in passivity all your life. Or you can get up and call out to Him who has your answer.

Your cry matters! The cries of God's people have always mattered. Moses was born and bred to lead the children of Israel out of Egypt into the Promised Land, yet God would never have placed him in that position had the Israelites not called out to Him. Exodus 2:23 tells us that *"the children of Israel groaned because of the bondage, and they cried out; and their cry came up to God because of the bondage"* (NKJV).

Once God heard their cry and acknowledged them (see Exod. 2:25), the very next verse begins the story of Moses' encounter with God at the burning bush (see Exod. 3:1). The promise of deliverance from Egypt had been made to Abraham hundreds of years earlier (see Gen. 15:14). But every promise in the Bible has a condition. If there had not been a cry from the people, the children of Israel might still be in Egypt to this day.

Your cry makes the difference; never discount it. It can change a child's life, redirect a family's destiny, determine whether a missionary lives or dies in a foreign land, or decide whether a nation rises or falls to communism or Islam.

When a burden falls upon your heart to cry out to the Lord, know that the answer is already starting to emerge. But know also that God is looking for intercessors throughout the land to take up the causes of His heart and bring them into the earth realm.

THE CRY OF INTERCESSION

A certain pastor was busy cleaning her house, when, all of a sudden, a burden to pray came upon her. She had a choice to make: she could continue cleaning or she could yield to the Holy Spirit who was telling her to get down and pray now!

The pastor stopped what she was doing and laid over the couch, travailing with mercy and compassion and crying out in intercession for the person the Lord had laid on her heart. She knew this person had been making bad decisions but had she said so to his face, he would have dismissed it out of hand.

As she cried out to God and yielded to Him in prayer, the burden for the person started to lift. She began to praise God, thanking Him for the peace that filled her soul. A couple of weeks later someone called her and said, "Did you hear what happened to So-and-So?" "So-and-So" was the very person she had prayed for that day!

The pastor answered, "No! What happened?"

They said, "He was totally delivered from drugs." Apparently, everyone in So-and-So's family went to the lake one day, while he stayed home and took a walk alone. During that walk he made an inspired decision to walk away from narcotics. He stopped taking drugs from that moment on. Needless to say, it changed his life—and the change didn't come from a conversation with anyone but God Himself.

The pastor exclaimed, "Really! What day did that happen?" The friend explained that it was the very same day and hour that the pastor had cried out to God.

Your cry matters. It can make all the difference in another person's life. You can talk and counsel someone for hours, but some things can only be done by the Spirit of the Living God.

And your prayers are the instruments here on earth that He uses.

LOCATE YOUR HEART

Are you like the church of Laodicea? Have you become lukewarm? (See Revelation 3:14-16.) It is time to stoke the fire underneath you and get the fire of your faith rekindled.

You need to know where you stand. Are you hot, cold, or lukewarm? God would rather have you be hot or cold. If you are lukewarm, He says He will *spew you out of* [His] *mouth!*" (Rev. 3:16 AMP).

This is not a time to be lukewarm. It is time to press through your problems. It is a season for you to get bold in the spirit. The woman with the issue of blood did that (see Matt. 9). When she touched Jesus' garment, she engaged Him. Her faith brought the power of God out of Jesus' garment and into her body. The power of God was always present but, because this woman pressed through—by faith—she received her healing.

Oral Roberts used to say that the people who believed they would be healed the moment he touched them always received their healing. This woman said she was going to get her healing and she did.

When you passionately seek after something to the point where you will boldly confess it out of your mouth, then you are going to receive what you are asking for.

The righteous cry out, and the Lord hears, and delivers them out of all their troubles. The Lord is near to those who have a broken heart, and saves such as have a contrite spirit. Many are the afflictions of the righteous, but the Lord delivers him out of them all (Psalm 34:17-19 NKJV).

You just need to move into a place of prayer and engage the enemy with a piercing cry that is a powerful instrument of battle. You *are* the righteous after all, and the enemy knows that. Of course, he would prefer you had permanent amnesia about who you are in Christ. That's why you must keep reminding yourself of your spiritual identity and hold your banner high!

There are many ways to "lift your banner" against the enemy: Gideon and his army used noise to confuse their opponent (see Judg. 7:19-21); Jehosephat used praise as his weapon on the front lines of battle (see 2 Chron. 20:20-22).

In both cases, God's people entered into His rest in order to see the victory. When you shout His praises, you demonstrate your belief that He has already answered your prayer. Faith allows you to enter His rest.

One minister I know encourages people to enter God's rest in a unique way. After he ministers his message about resting in God, he has the people lie down on the pews and relax. Then, as the people remain in this attitude of rest, he lays his hands on them.

God has promised rest to His people and requires us to enter that rest. His rest is not a waste of time; it is a benefit of trusting Him. The writer of Hebrews emphasizes the importance of the promise:

Let us therefore fear, lest, a promise being left us of entering into His rest, any of you should seem

to come short of it. For we which have believed do
enter into rest... (Hebrews 4:1,3).

Rest is faith-based. If you do not rest in Him, you will continually strive to "make things happen" on your own. This exhausting effort will grate on your spirit and cause you to develop tunnel vision. Instead of relieving stress, you will generate *more* stress.

To rest, on the other hand, is to wait upon the Lord. Instead of striving, you will take the opposite action: you will cry out to the One who is able to accomplish what your flesh cannot. Crying is a release from your spirit that connects you to God.

God hears when you cry, especially if you are pleading with Him to rectify an injustice. Perhaps your spouse has committed adultery; maybe someone has stolen your money or cheated you out of a promotion. Whatever the injustice, if you take your anger or sorrow out on the offender, any so-called benefit you gain will be temporal, at best. Turn the situation and the offender over to God. *"Vengeance is mine; I **will** repay, saith the Lord"* (Rom. 12:19, emphasis added). He will get the job done for you better than you could have ever done it yourself. (He can turn hearts and minds around in the most amazing ways.) But you have to cast the care on Him, believing He is well able to handle it.

My wife Mary was asked to be part of an all-news radio station that was starting up in Las Vegas, Nevada, before we were married. She had learned the broadcast journalism "ropes" as a radio news reporter at a large Santa Barbara, California, station. Because she was becoming so accomplished in her field, she had even been asked to audition for a larger network station in Washington, D.C.

When Mary started the Las Vegas job, the persecution started too. Stories that were normally a breeze for her to write became a real grind due to criticism from another female broadcaster named Gail. My wife had never met Gail before, but her counterpart was a stickler for details. She picked apart Mary's stories to the point of almost getting her fired. Mary couldn't believe what was happening, because she'd had an excellent reputation up to that point.

In spite of the pressure, Mary continued to work and put her best foot forward on the job. It was almost as though the enemy was trying to get her to leave Las Vegas before she could really get started—and certainly before effective Christian laborers would cross her path and witness to her.

Some time later, Mary became a News Director at another Las Vegas radio station. By this time she had accepted Jesus as her personal Lord and Savior. Meanwhile, Gail had become a news anchor on the local television station. Amazingly, Gail also had gotten saved!

After a chance meeting where Mary and Gail laughed about their earlier conflict, and decided to meet regularly for prayer. They would also arrange to connect at interviews they were doing around town. As a result of the prayer, the hostility between them dissolved. Even more importantly, they began witnessing effectively to the many celebrities who came through Las Vegas. Ronald Reagan, Willie Nelson, and Jane Fonda were among the luminaries to whom they had an opportunity to present the Gospel. Although Reagan was already a Christian, as they learned, he was glad to find members of the news media who were not against him because of his faith.

The way Mary and Gail accomplished their outreach was simple. After fulfilling their obligations to capture the story for their respective stations, they would turn off their microphones and start witnessing to their interviewees.

Not long after these developments, the disc jockey at Mary's radio station became interested in Gail. He also got saved and all three of them started attending the same church. Gail ended up marrying the disc jockey. Mary was one of her bridesmaids.

The Lord managed to salvage that relationship and turn it around to accomplish great good. What a profound change God brought: instead of having her stories ripped apart by a co-worker, Mary became one of Gail's closest friends at the time and a bridesmaid in her wedding—a friend with whom she would share ministry to others. This was a reconciliation only the Lord could have done by His Spirit.

SUMMARY

1. Your peace and joy demonstrate to the enemy that, because of God, you have the upper hand and are not moved by Satan's machinations.

2. Persevere through hard times and never quit praying. You are closer to your breakthrough than you think.

3. When Jesus speaks to your heart and tells you to get going, He is saying that you are in a kairos moment of favor on your life.

4. Your cry matters! God would never have appointed Moses to lead the Israelites out of Egypt had the people not cried out to Him.

5. To rest is to wait upon the Lord. Instead of striving, cry out to the One who is able to accomplish what your flesh cannot.

CHAPTER FOUR

YOUR VOICE
MUST SPEAK

The cry of your heart is a prayer that goes beyond words. When that cry comes out of your mouth, it is as if your spirit itself is touching the heart of God. This is not a silent prayer; it is the voice of a desperate intercessor ready to make his case before almighty God, no matter what the cost.

Isaiah 58:1 says, *"Cry aloud, spare not, lift up thy voice like a trumpet...."* God gave you a voice primarily to worship and communicate with Him. Although millions never do that, there is a remnant of those who do. God is always looking for those people, because it is the few who are willing to stand in the gap who will make the difference as to whether a battle is won or lost.

Man was given a powerful gift of speech; in Genesis 2:19, God allowed him to name all the birds, animals, and living creatures. But no creature can speak the way man can. When man opens his mouth and talks to God, he takes hold of life itself. A human being is a spirit, has a soul, and lives in a body. His spirit and soul will live for eternity; the body will stay on earth.

God does not just hand us this ability without showing us how speech works. He gives us detailed instructions. There is more mention on the power of speech in the Jewish Torah than there is about any other bodily function.

God's guidance about speech is important, because as long as you are on this earth, you are choosing words which will cause you to live in Heaven or hell for eternity. It is up to you to decide with whose side you will align yourself.

Yes! Your future *is* determined by your tongue. Your today is the sum total of the words you spoke in your yesterdays. Jesus certainly knew how important it was for us to understand this truth; He demonstrated the power of the tongue when he cursed the fig tree. The very next day after He spoke to the fig tree, it withered and died. (See Mark 11:13,20.)

David also understood the connection between the tongue and life. He said, *"Set a watch, O Lord, before my mouth; keep the door of my lips"* (Ps. 141:3). Proverbs 18:21 tells us: *"Death and life are in the power of the tongue...."*

It is hard to imagine how powerful your words are, but if you put this truth into practice long enough, you will see results. If you speak healing, it will bring you life; but talking about this or that disease and complaining about how it is affecting your body can bring only death.

Certain kinds of words produce certain types of results. According to Proverbs 16:24 *"pleasant words are as an honeycomb, sweet to the soul* [your mind, will, and emotions] *and health to your bones."* When we trust God, we will take His Word and put it in our hearts. Proverbs 3:8 says that trust in His ways *"is health to thy navel, and marrow to thy bones."*

Only man gets to choose where he will live for eternity. You make that choice here on earth when you decide whether you will receive Jesus as your Lord and Savior. If you think you can wait to choose Him after you die, you will find that you have waited too long.

When you make a decision to ask Jesus into your heart, your spirit is speaking. Not only does your spirit speak, it also cries out using your voice. God's people have cried out this way for centuries. When no one else would listen, John the Baptist cried in the wilderness saying, *"I am the voice of one crying in the wilderness, Make straight the way of the Lord, as said the prophet Esaias"* (John 1:23).

God heard John, despite the fact that John had no clothing or food except for camels' hair, locusts, and wild honey. He didn't have angels, shepherds, or wise men heralding his birth. He only had a cry of the Spirit. Yet, with one cry, he moved the whole world from the wilderness.

God was crying through John. It was His Spirit pleading for the earth to repent. The earth was moved by the mountain man's call for repentance: *"Repent ye, for the kingdom of heaven is at hand"* (Matt. 3:2).

Multitudes were moved and circumstances were changed though John's cry. Conviction fell upon many; people's hearts were purged and they found new purpose in life. The people were baptized in the Jordan River and confessed their sins.

> ... *The word of God came unto John the son of Zacharias in the wilderness. And he came into all the country about the Jordan, preaching the baptism of repentance for the remission of sins* (Luke 3:2-3).

John was alone with God when he received His Word. You need, at times, to be in a secluded place with Him to receive His mind, thoughts, and impressions about what people need and what He is leading you to do. John was extraordinary; he was a holy man who dared to be alone with God. God had his heart in such a way that John could express his cry—a cry for the whole land. John had a heart to plead for the sins of the people. Having been filled with the Spirit from his mother's womb (see Luke 1:15), he was consumed with the call to move in the perfect will of God.

John (meaning "favored one") was direct, upright, and clear in his message. God gave him a cry for repentance. We need that cry today. Repentance is a radical change of mind, direction, and action. This is what we must seek in order to change our world. The world is steeped in sin, yet we know that where sin abounds, grace abounds even more (see Rom. 5:20).

That grace will abound in your cry. It abounded in John the Baptist's cry. Because John's message prepared the way, Jesus had a path to walk on in the Spirit. He would be received because people were expecting Him. John had come and shaved off the sharp edges of the unrepentant hearts. He had a bare-bones, no-holds-barred approach to ministry: what you saw and heard was what you got with this rugged forerunner.

"John came neither eating nor drinking..." (Matt. 11:18). The only freedom John had was being in the presence of God in the wilderness. That was where he received the cry of repentance—the preparation needed for redemption. Jesus could not come until the people changed their minds. Then they would also change their ways.

It is going to take a spirit of boldness to really cry out to God. Your cry must be passionate and from the depths of your innermost being. It begins with a working of the Spirit in you. Then God can work through you to save others. Give way to the Lord's leadings in your life, even to His moving, brooding, and promptings. Be a person God can depend upon to flow in the supernatural, someone who is courageous and does exploits, someone consumed with and gripped by Him.

God has a good plan for your life; He will reveal it to you in His presence. God's Word says that He will show you the path of life. He says you will find fullness of joy in His presence and eternal pleasures at His right hand. (See Psalm 16:11.)

Do the last thing God told you to do and He will show you the next thing He has planned for your life. The enemy will be put to flight as you walk in God's perfect will. Even those around you will acknowledge that the Lord is leading you.

FACE THE PROBLEM; OPEN YOUR MOUTH

Young David had enormous problems confronting him at an early age. Imagine being a shepherd boy facing a huge giant in the valley between two warring armies! (See First Samuel 17.)

The battle between David and Goliath was not just about the two of them; it was about the future of nations and would determine the fate of thousands of people. One army would become the champion; one would become slave to the victor.

That is what you must realize when you are in a battle. It is not just about you; it is about you allowing God's plan to work through your life to get the victory for all the generations to come after you. It is a matter of choosing this day whom you will serve (see Josh. 24:15) *and* knowing you are not the only one who will be affected by your decision.

What did David do when he faced Goliath? He opened his mouth, spoke words of victory, and ran at the giant. David had a cry in his heart. He didn't just sit there and look at the monster of a man coming at him. No! David ran toward the giant! David didn't just sit there with King Saul, Israel's army, and his mocking brothers; David took action.

That was no small feat. Consider these facts: Goliath was 13 feet tall; he was covered in a coat of armor weighing 278 pounds (probably twice David's weight); this was in addition to his own weight which could have been between 400 and 600 pounds.[1] The sight of this giant would have been enough to back down the bravest opponent!

If David had stopped to consider his adversary's dimensions and weaponry, he could have easily turned and fled—but not this ruddy young warrior. Holy Ghost boldness rose up in David, and with good reason. First of all, he recognized that Goliath was defying Almighty God. David knew he had a blood covenant with God and he knew God could not fail him. Besides that, the Lord had already brought him through encounters with a lion and a bear who were after his sheep—and David prevailed.

David had three more huge incentives for killing this giant. First, David would receive great riches. Second, he would marry the king's daughter; that would position him even more closely to the throne. Finally, he and his family would be exempt from taxes and military service all their lives.

But before David could even have a chance at being Israel's champion, he had to convince King Saul of his ability to carry out the plan. He courageously told the king of his qualifications:

> *Thy servant slew both the lion and the bear: and this uncircumcised Philistine shall be as one of them, seeing he hath defied the armies of the living God* (1 Samuel 17:36).

In other words, David said, "Who does this character Goliath think he is? He may be big, but he is not bigger than God."

Any enemy in your life is to be viewed the same way. Whatever is opposing you is not bigger than the Lord.

David cried out to a living God whom he knew had answered

him many times before. David had even retrieved the lambs the lion and the bear had tried to eat, snatching them right out of the predators' mouths! This battle with Goliath would be no different, because David had faith in a God who never let him down.

David's faith never wavered—not even when Goliath came out on the battlefield, looked at David, and laughed at what he saw.

> *And when the Philistine looked about, and saw David, he disdained him: for he was but a youth, and ruddy, and of a fair countenance* (1 Samuel 17:42).

For David to be a shepherd boy delivering food to his soldier brothers meant that he was under the enlistment age of 20 required by Israel's army. He had not been drafted, much less gone to boot camp—and he still looked like a child! The giant must have thought, *This kid is a pushover.* Goliath was insulted that Israel had not sent him a more worthy opponent.

Sometimes, like David, we must have both childlike faith to resist the enemy's onslaughts and godly wisdom enough to know the battle is not ours, but the Lord's. Goliath told David in essence, "Get over here, you don't have a chance," and then threatened to feed David's flesh to wild animals (see 1 Sam. 17:44).

But David was full of courage and promptly answered his cocky opponent. Your biggest mistake is to keep silent when the devil is testing you. To win you must declare the final outcome of victory to his face before it manifests, and you have to do it boldly, without hesitation. That is exactly what David did.

> *Then said David to the Philistine, Thou comest to me with a sword, and with a spear, and with a*

shield: but I come to thee in the name of the Lord of hosts, the God of the armies of Israel, whom thou hast defied. (1 Samuel 17:45).

In other words, David said, "Goliath, you are coming at me with natural weapons, but I am coming back at you with supernatural weapons that will win every time!" David went on to foretell his victory:

This day will the Lord deliver thee into mine hand; and I will smite thee, and take thine head from thee....And all this assembly shall know that the Lord saveth not with sword and spear: for the battle is the Lord's, and He will give you into our hands (1 Samuel 17:46-47).

Sometimes you just have to declare the future to the enemy no matter what threats he makes against you. There is an audience of people around you watching to see how you are going to react in this situation. Are you going to cower in fear or cry out in faith?

The giant was a fully-armed, huge specimen of a human being and he chose to rest in a seated position during David's brave declarations of victory. He did not stay down for long. *"... The Philistine arose, and came and drew nigh to meet David..."* (1 Sam. 17:48).

David's bold prophetic statements motivated Goliath to get up on his feet and come after the outspoken teenager. But that didn't stop David. Instead, First Samuel 17:48 goes on to tell us that *"David hasted"* toward his adversary. The Hebrew word for "hasted" here is *mahar,* which means "to be liquid or flow easily...to hurry; or act promptly"[2] or "go swiftly like a charging lion."[3]

Before the slow-thinking giant figured out what was going

on, David struck him with a stone slung at his forehead. You might wonder how it is possible for one smooth stone to kill a 13-foot tall giant. In part, David's plan worked because he was prepared. He did not come at the Philistine empty-handed. David selected five smooth stones from the brook before he even approached his enemy. All David had to do was to pick out the right stone when the time came.

In those days, shepherds always kept stones ready. They didn't wait for an emergency to arise before finding a stone. They selected smooth, round stones that would hit their mark without veering off-course.

Preparedness is key. You can't just stand against the enemy empty-handed; you must be positioned to act when the time is right. At the Mount of Temptation, where the devil threatened Jesus, the Lord was ready with His answer to the enemy's provocations before the battle of words began.

Preparedness increases confidence in battle. David's readiness with his weapon helped him have the extra measure of assurance he needed to defeat the enemy. Preparation will help you to get the victory.

History records the Israelite's rock-slinging expertise:

> Men of Israel were adept at slinging stones and many hundreds would throw at a hairbreadth and never miss. David must have been among the best who used a sling. Much practice was required in this, but once it was mastered, it could be as deadly as a musket or a bow. The Achaeans were so expert that they principally used slings in warfare, and by long practice from childhood could hit any spot they aimed at.[4]

Maybe it is time for you to aim your slingshot at the enemy's head using a passionate cry from your heart. You have prayed, you have declared, you continue to decree. But God is waiting for passion. After all, James says. *"The **effectual fervent** prayer of a righteous man availeth **much**"* (James 5:16, emphasis added). The words *effectual fervent* here are translated with the single Greek word *energeo*. Another translation could describe "a prayer of a just man wrought in him by divine energy."

To be effective, our prayers need to be not only Word-based, but also powered by the key ingredient of divine energy. You can put a pan of water on the stove, but unless you turn on the heat, the water will never boil. In order to get your prayers moving in the right direction, you must be fervent. You must be passionate.

George Mueller was another great man of faith who established an orphan house in England in the early 19th century entirely by prayer and faith and crying out to God in sincerity.

While waiting before the Lord to determine His will as to whether Mueller was the person to actually do this work, the Lord dropped Psalm 81:10 into his heart, *"...open thy mouth wide, and I will fill it."* In other words the Lord wanted Mueller to enlarge his tents, strengthen his stakes, and ask God for big things. Mueller realized that he had not actually asked God for what he wanted, but only whether it was the Lord's will to establish the orphanage. His praying immediately took a different track. His heart changed to embrace the work and ask for big things: a house to take care of the children, 1,000 pounds to start the work with, and the right people to take care of the orphans. As soon as God's will in the matter was settled, the Lord gave him definite directives to get the job done.

Like Nehemiah of old, Mueller wanted to rebuild the wall for God. Once he saw God was in the details, he started opening his mouth wide and asking for specifics. He knew there was no way in the natural for him to obtain any of these things, but he relied on God's faithfulness.[5]

Writings from George Mueller's narratives at this time are revealing:

> December 10, 1835—This morning I received a letter, in which a brother and sister wrote thus:— "We propose ourselves for the service of the intended Orphan-House, if you think us qualified for it; also to give up all the furniture . . . which the Lord has given us, for its use; and to this without receiving any salary whatever; believing that if it be the will of the Lord to employ us, He will supply all our needs . . . ."

> Dec. 13—A brother was influenced this day to give 4s. per week, or £10 8s. yearly, as long as the Lord gives the means; 8s was given by him as two weeks' subscriptions.

> Dec. 17—I was rather cast down last evening and this morning about the matter, questioning whether I ought to be engaged in this way, and was led to ask the Lord to give me some further encouragement. Soon after were sent by a brother two pieces of print, [including some] calico, four pieces of lining about four yards altogether, a sheet and a yard measure. This evening another brother brought a clothes horse, three frocks, four pinafores, six handkerchiefs he also brought 3s. 6d. given to him by three different individuals. At the same time he told me that it had been put into the heart of an individual to send tomorrow £100.

> June 15, 1837—To-day I gave myself once more earnestly to prayer respecting the remainder of the £1,000. This evening £5 was given, so that now the whole sum is made up. To the glory of God, whose I am, and whom I serve, I would state again, that every shilling of this money, and all the articles of clothing and furniture, which have been mentioned in the foregoing pages, have been given to me, *without one single individual having been asked by me for anything.*"[6]

George Mueller was passionate in his calling and in his cry to God. The Lord gave you that same passion with which to speak up and cry out. He also sent His Son Jesus to cover you with the precious Blood that He shed on the cross. You can rely on that Blood covering to bring victory against the enemy. Revelation 12:11 says that those who are accused by satan *"overcame him by the blood of the Lamb, and by the word of their testimony...."*

The word of your testimony, your speaking up and declaring what God has done in your life, undermines satanic opposition. Mueller never asked people for anything, but he did testify and glorify God before and after the Lord blessed him.

Your testimony does more than glorify God; it also builds you up. The more you look the enemy in the eye and declare who you are in Christ, the more it becomes a reality in your life. The more you rehearse past victories and decree future triumphs in the face of a trial, the more the pressure subsides.

So declare the truth about yourself and about the faithfulness of God to keep His promises. Speak it out loud. Every time the enemy lies to you, cancel it out with God's Word. Every time you feel defeated, replace the feeling with a declaration of your faith in the power of the Blood to overcome. Stand strong on the rock of what God says—it will support you and help you stand through every storm.

God has a plan for your life. However, that plan cannot come to pass until it is spoken. God chose to allow His only-begotten Son to be born, to live, to die, and to be resurrected so He could restore man to his rightful place. God saw that plan with His own eyes of faith.

But, even God had to speak the plan into existence (see Gen. 3:15). And since *"faith is the substance of things hoped for, the evidence of things not seen"* (Heb. 11:1), God created the substance called "faith" to provide for us the evidence—the assurance that His plan would come to pass.

SUMMARY

1. The few who are willing to stand in the gap praying will make the difference between a battle won and a battle lost.

2. Your future is determined by your tongue; therefore, your today is the sum total of the words you spoke in your yesterdays.

3. Your cry must be passionate and from the depths of your innermost being. It begins with a working of the Spirit in you. Then God can work through you to save others.

4. Do the last thing God told you to do and He will show you the next thing He has planned for your life.

5. When the enemy lies to you, cancel it out with the truth of God's Word. Every time you feel defeated, replace the feeling with a declaration of your faith in the power of the Blood to overcome.

CHAPTER FIVE

MERCY COMES
FIRST

Hear, O Lord, when I cry with my voice! Have mercy also upon me, and answer me. When You said, "Seek My face," my heart said to You, "Your face, Lord, I will seek" (Psalm 27:7-8 NKJV).

Mercy is a cry that says, "God, please don't give them what they deserve." When you decide to be merciful, you are deciding to be lenient when you have every right to judge.

Unfortunately, religion is more concerned with judgment than with mercy because religion is law-oriented. But relationship is love-oriented.

God is a God of love; He is not critical toward you. But He will allow what you allow. If you allow strife, bickering, and gossip to be a part of your everyday life, these works of the flesh will separate you from God's best for your life. If you participate in adultery, fornication, or drunkenness, you will create a gap between yourself and the Lord. He didn't do it, you did it.

Repent and make a decision to change. Walk in love. Don't let your prayers be contaminated with criticism and backbiting attitudes; remember, you reap what you sow every single time. It is a law of the universe; He has created the universe and all of its laws. Those laws are already in place. When you throw a ball up in the air, gravity will bring it down; and every time you sow, you put a natural law into effect.

After God redeemed Jonah from the belly of the whale, Jonah got back to his original pre-whale assignment and went and preached repentance to Nineveh. Then when Jonah realized God actually wanted to save the whole city, he got mad at Him. This was after Jonah himself had been rescued from certain demise in the whale's belly!

Did Jonah's memory get fogged by the fish's digestive juices? He thought the people of Nineveh were underserving of God's mercy, but neither did he deserve to be rescued from the whale's belly! He had almost caused a whole ship and its crew to be capsized in a storm because of his backsliding ways. Had he not admitted that he was the reason they were in the storm, they might have all perished.

When people repent, God turns and pours out His mercy on them. We also need to pour out mercy when others change their minds—especially when they don't deserve mercy. None of us deserves such a great salvation, but the Lord has given it to us anyway. If all the angels in Heaven rejoice over one sinner who gets saved, we should rejoice, too.

Ask the Lord to remove every judgmental attitude from your

heart. Consider how *"mercy triumphs over judgment"* (James 2:13). James is saying that, because we have been justified by grace, we are now under the mercy of the New Testament. We are no longer under the legal restraints of the Old Covenant.

There is no mercy under the law. But His grace will triumph over the law because the demands of the law have been met. The lawbreakers are justified through faith. God's grace and mercy take us to the winning side.

THE CRY RESTORED

The Church has lost its cry. We don't know how to cry anymore. We cry out of knowledge, but not out of passion. The Lord spoke to my heart; He said that He is coming and is going to put the cry back inside us. He is going to put a cry of mercy in you for your family, your city, your nation, the troops, and the Church.

Sometimes you will see people in prayer meetings who are moved by the Holy Spirit to weep for a person, situation, or nation. God places great value on your tears; He wants to hear your heart, not your head. He wants us to feel what the people we are praying for are feeling, to identify with their pain. When you are weeping in prayer like this, it is much more than emotional tears; it is a powerful heartfelt gesture of worship to Him.

Once, when we were ministering throughout Europe, an opportunity came to pray for a woman with terminal cancer. By that time, we had preached 23 services over a two-week period in Belgium and France. Some of the immigrant churches there are so hungry for a move of God that they will worship for two hours and want you to preach for another three hours. I was getting a little weary. I can keep up with the best of them, but night after night of long services was beginning to get to me physically. But the cry that God is putting inside us is filled with compassion. His passion in us overcomes weariness and weakness.

A pastor came to us after a service, and said, "There is a 38-year-old woman across town in the hospital. She has uterine cancer and has never been able to have a child. The cancer is going to kill her because it is spreading in her body. Would you go over to the hospital and pray for her?"

"I'll let you know," I hastily responded. My wife and I walked away and then I started complaining. I said, "There are a lot of people sick in the hospital. We have probably already prayed for 300 people during these meetings. There will always be sick people in the hospital who need prayer."

Have you ever complained? We all have at one time or another. So my wife and I walked back to our hotel and into the elevator. The elevator doors closed and, all of a sudden, the Lord spoke to me. He said, "Son, what if she were your daughter? This woman is My daughter."

My prideful heart melted before His still small voice, "Well, Lord, if she were my daughter, I wouldn't care how far it might be, or how tired I was. Lord, please forgive me."

I stood in that elevator and began to weep before the Lord and in that weeping God released in me an anointing to take to that hospital. That afternoon, we got on the Paris Metro (the French subway) to go to the hospital. The Metro can whisk you across Paris in 30 to 40 minutes. Because of the cars, pedestrians, and motorcycles jamming the streets, making the same trip above-ground can take several hours.

When we walked into that hospital room, there lay this 38-year-old woman from the former Belgian Congo. She had never met us before. We told her who we were and said, "We have come in the Name of the Lord Jesus and we are going to lay hands on you. That sickness, that disease, is going to leave your body."

We proceeded to pray and the power of God hit her so hard, she began weeping. She was healed in Jesus' name. The cry will spark compassion in your heart when you are faced with people in need. The only reason we lack compassion for people is because we have lost the cry.

Moses was an amazing intercessor, full of mercy. No matter how miserable and complaining and outright rebellious the children of Israel were, he stuck up for them in front of God— even when they turned against him. You would think Moses would have wanted to wash his hands of the whole group and go back to the peaceful shepherd's life he had shared with his wife and father-in-law in the desert. At the very least, you would think Moses would have agreed with God's complaints against the people, and said, "Go ahead, Lord, throw down fire from Heaven and destroy them with one breath from Your nostrils."

But not Moses! Instead...

> ...Moses returned to the Lord and said, "Oh, these people have committed a great sin, and have made for themselves a god of gold! Yet now, if You will forgive their sin—but if not, I pray, blot me out of Your book which You have written (Exodus 32:31-32 NKJV).

Moses said, "Lord, if You are going to wipe them out, wipe me out too, because I am with these people." The Lord wants us to seek His agenda before we seek our own. And He offers great rewards for doing so; as you seek first His Kingdom, *all these things shall be added unto you* (Matt. 6:33).

In other words, don't seek the things, seek His will for your life. Let Him show you your gifts and callings and you will be a great teacher, CEO, singer, politician, worshiper, minister, evangelist, missionary, engineer, computer technician, or housewife for His glory. Be the best at what you can be and let God shine through you with mercy and kindness toward others. Watch Him add everything you need to your life. You reach out with His love to others, and He reaches out with His love and provision back to you.

Once you have a heart motivated by compassion for others, a heart that cries out for His mercy, He will allow you to see more deeply into people's motivations and methods. When you are not sitting in judgment of them, He will show you how to demolish strongholds in their lives.

I remember another time when we were walking down the streets of Brussels on our way to a bakery. There are wonderful bakeries in Belgium, especially for goods made with chocolate.

In Europe, many people beg on the side of the road. Most of them are elderly women who sit there with children. Hundreds of people walk by them every day. They just sit there, hoping someone will drop a coin in their lap.

There we were, walking down this street, when, all of a sudden, I spotted this 16-year-old boy. He was wearing a pair of Levis, but they were dirty and torn and had seen better days. It was unusual to see a young man sitting there begging. Most of the beggars were older, more disheveled and forlorn.

It was obvious that this teen was very depressed. He didn't want to look anyone in the eye. He just sat there begging with a plastic cup that had a ragged top edge. As I walked by, the Lord spoke to me and said, "Son, I want to show compassion to that young man."

I said, "Lord, what do You want me to do?"

He said, "I want you to go into that bakery and get a brand-new cup. I want you to fill it with money and I want you to put it back in his hands."

So I put the brand-new cup with all that money right into the young man's hand. All of a sudden, he looked up at me. I cannot describe the look he had in his eyes. I didn't know what his situation was; for all I knew, he had been kicked out of his home or verbally abused by his father. Maybe he lived with his sick mother or had some kind of disease. What I do know is that he looked up at me and tears began to roll out of his eyes. I couldn't say anything because I could not speak French. But when I left that young boy, I can tell you for certain that he was struck by that small gesture for eternity. He will never forget that day for the rest of his life.

When God begins to put the cry back in your heart, you will have compassion for people. You won't be like the multitudes who say in their hearts, "Just don't bother me right now." Instead, you will begin to see things through the eyes of the Master. The heart of the Good Samaritan will come on you and you will act out that compassion. This is the cry we must have—for the nations, for the Body of Christ, and for humanity in general. If we don't have a cry, we will cry.

"... *You received the spirit of sonship. And by Him we cry 'Abba, Father'*" (Rom. 8:15 NIV). I believe that what this verse is talking about is a spirit of prayer resting on a person. It's not about someone who is merely reciting prayers by rote, but someone who is truly yearning to touch the heart of God. That's when the Holy Spirit comes through us "crying"—meaning He is "crying out to the Father" on our behalf.

In Galatians 4:6, Paul writes *"Because you are sons, God sent the Spirit of His Son into our hearts, the Spirit who calls out, 'Abba, Father'"* (NIV). In Romans 8:15 we are the ones who cry, *"Abba, Father"* by means of the Holy Spirit. But in the Galatians passage, it is the Holy Spirit within us who cries, *"Abba, Father."*

The Holy Spirit wants to pray His perfect plan for your life through you. When He cries to the Father on your behalf, He works out every single detail of your life—the same minute details He heard the Father plan out at the foundations of the earth. When God designed creation, your name was there. He laid out a perfect plan for your personal life. The Holy Spirit was part of that process and He listened to God delineate every facet. He planned your birth, family, ministry, business, and every aspect of your redemption.

The Holy Spirit is the perfect Person to represent His plan for your life since He was there when God created it. As soon as you made the decision to become born again, the Holy Spirit consented to take up residence within your spirit and offer His "services" to you.

One of the main benefits the Holy Spirit provides is to pray for you. All fruitfulness in your spirit flows out of intimacy with the Holy Spirit. That is why it is so important to develop and strengthen your relationship with Him. When you allow distractions to get in the way of your time with Him, the fruitfulness that springs from prayer fades and indifference sets in.

We have lost the cry, we have become hardened. Do you know why? It is because we watch media that inundate our senses and sear our consciences with the "hot irons" of violence, sex, and negativity. We watch TV, movie, and video game characters getting their heads slashed off; we see their bodies mutilated so often that it does not affect us anymore. We have become desensitized and indifferent.

We cry out of religion rather than relationship. But God does not want to hear your professional prayers. He wants to hear your heart. God wants to put that cry back into your life, so that when you go someplace with Him, you will begin to weep; you'll begin to pour out your heart for your loved ones, for the daughter who was raised in the Church, but has strayed away. You'll have a cry for that relative who is out there on drugs and needs to know the Lord. You'll have a cry for the ministry and for this nation.

God is bringing us into a season of fruitfulness. The barren land is going to become fruitful through your heart cry, through your willingness to lay your life down for a world that is desperate for your prayers. But don't try to gather the harvest until you have won the war. First you must clear the land and take territory. Then you plant your seeds, and finally, you reap the harvest. There is a day of breakthrough coming; it will be as Isaiah 2:4 says:

> *He will judge between the nations and will settle disputes for many peoples. They will beat their swords into plowshares and their spears into pruning hooks. Nation will not take up sword against nation, nor will they train for war anymore* (NIV).

A day is coming when the presence of God will be so prevalent throughout the earth that breakthrough will be inevitable. We will no longer need to cry out because the ripened fruit will be right there in front of us. We will take up our plowshares and begin harvesting.

SUMMARY

1. When we repent, God pours out His mercy on us. When others repent, we need to do the same.

2. Ask the Lord to reveal and remove any judgmental attitudes that are in your heart; then refuse to re-adopt them.

3. The cry will spark compassion in your heart; it will guide you when you are faced with people in need.

4. The Holy Spirit wants to pray through you God's perfect plan for your life. Allow Him to work out the details He heard from the Father at the foundations of the earth.

5. Prevent distractions from stealing your time with Him and you'll promote the fruitfulness that springs from prayer.

CHAPTER SIX

REPENTANCE BRINGS
FREEDOM

The word *repent* simply means "to think again." The prefix *re* in Latin means "again"; *pentare* means "to think." So when you repent you are making a decision to change your thinking.

People often think repentance is a painful and difficult choice. But when you change your thinking, it has a domino effect, causing everything else to change in its wake. The way you act, the way you talk, what you read, and what you watch— all are transformed, because your desires change.

A lot of times we just don't realize how horrifying and destructive sin can be. In order to have a cry in our hearts, we must be grateful for what Jesus did for us on the cross to forgive our sins.

You might say, "But I thanked Him years ago." Yes, but don't lose sight of that gratitude just because you have gone down the road a ways. Don't allow your heart to become indifferent to your salvation or to the world around you. Come to Him on a daily basis with a repentant spirit.

When Isaiah recognized the way he really was, he wasted no time in cleaning up his heart. Isaiah cried out to God:

> *Woe is me! for I am undone; because I am a man of unclean lips, and I dwell in the midst of a people of unclean lips: for mine eyes have seen the King, the Lord of hosts* (Isaiah 6:5).

Isaiah saw how sin had affected him and wanted to get clean again. He knew he was off course and wanted to get back on track.

It is easy to get off course only a few degrees and then wonder why things are not working in our lives. Once we see the necessity of correcting our own thinking and repenting of sin, we have a much greater sense of urgency to rescue others from sin.

Isaiah was not primarily concerned with other people missing the mark. He had to clean up himself first; then he could help others. Like the apostle Paul said, *"I keep under my body, and bring it into subjection: lest that by any means, when I have preached to others, I myself should be a castaway"* (1 Cor. 9:27). The word *keep* here means "to strike one under the eyes; to beat black and blue."[1]

Paul was saying that he was beating his body black and blue, figuratively speaking, to bring it under control. Paul considered his body an "enemy with which he must contend in mortal combat to keep it under control by self-denial, abstinence, and…mortification."[2] He knew it was vital to keep his body obedient to his spirit, not allowing his "soul to be a slave of the body."[3]

Paul did this continually to make sure that after he preached he did not become a "castaway." The word *castaway* there means to become Christless and literally "rejected."[4]

Once we make the decision to take control of our flesh with the help of the Holy Spirit, we have the ability to turn to a whole generation of people around us. We can help them one by one as the Lord leads them across our paths. That is true discipleship, being a real follower of Christ. When you get a sense of the Presence of the wonderful spotless Lamb of God who can save everyone from their sin, you want to be used by Him to reach those who are lost.

You must value your relationship with Him and honor Him. This is not a church thing. This is a love you must value above all. There are so many ungrateful Christians. We need to realize that we can never know the full magnitude of this great salvation. That realization will help us to be grateful to God.

Before God can put the cry back into your heart you are going to have to ask Him to forgive you, saying, "God forgive me. I am grateful and thankful. I have made mistakes. People have had to ask me to go to church, Lord, and I declined their invitations. And when I do go, I don't take my Bible along. I have not been giving my tithes and offerings like I used to. I have the money, but I don't give it. Forgive me, Lord. Everything I have exists because You have allowed me to walk in it. All that I have is Yours. I have been selfish. I have not done my part. I ask You to forgive me. I ask You to forgive me for the disrespect that I have shown You and others. No wonder people don't want to get saved. What they see in me won't attract them to You. Forgive me, Father."

Once you repent, it is not hard to die to the fleshly desires you used to have. By your very decision to "think again," you have set positive change in motion. With the Holy Spirit in charge of your life, former desires just do not have the draw and hold on you.

The repentant heart also desires purity. Before God can put this cry in your heart you must have a clean heart, the kind of heart for which David cried out to the Lord: *"Create in me a clean heart, O God; and renew a right spirit within me"* (Ps. 51:10). Just repent of the way you have been acting and ask God to forgive you.

God can change a heart in a moment. Unfortunately, people often run to the front of the church in an emotional response to an altar call, as though thinking that one altar call will fix everything that is wrong in their lives. No doubt, an altar call can be a new beginning, but just because you leave your sins at the altar doesn't mean the enemy isn't going to try to lure you to pick them up again.

It is great to repent and make a commitment to God not to miss the mark again. But it is also important not to overlook the main problem: the root of the situation, the spiritual road-blocks that remain hidden in darkness. These must be uncovered and removed.

That is where the washing of the water of the Word comes in. You have to take the Bible and wash your mind with it daily. If you want to grow and mature into the fullness of the person you are in Christ, you must build up a defensive wall against sin.

You must also build up a good offense. After all, a key part of the armor of God is the sword of the Spirit. You don't use a sword strictly for defense. If you expect to win the fight against your adversary on this earth, you must use your sword offensively as well. Jesus was on the offense when He spoke to the enemy on the Mount of Temptation. The enemy finally gave up because of Jesus' persistence.

Another key to seeing roots uncovered and removed is to consistently and persistently pray in other tongues. Your human spirit is permanently edified when you pray in other tongues. Still, once roots are uncovered and removed, you will need to put to death the deeds of the flesh—on a daily basis. When you are filled with the Holy Spirit with the evidence of speaking in tongues, be faithful to *use* the gift He has given you. When you do, you will realize lasting change in your life.

It is amazing that people think they can change by themselves without the Lord. This is a deceptive form of New Age thinking; it tries to make *self* bigger and greater than God. Real change—permanent change—only comes through intimacy with the Holy Spirit.

All your life, your mind has been trained to believe that you can control yourself by being strong-willed. But, hard as you try, you cannot break bad habits through the strength of your own will. The Holy Spirit living inside of you is the agent of change.

When you release His Spirit inside of you through prayer and supplication, you will be able to put to death the deeds of the flesh. You cannot do that on your own.

The Holy Spirit is God's agent here on earth and He wants to pray through you. But He is a gentleman and will not move unless you give Him permission and yield yourself to Him. Then, once your flesh and self-life have been subdued, the Man of Compassion, Jesus Himself, will start to take first place in your life.

The enemy fights so hard to see that people do not get filled with the Spirit because he knows they will no longer yield to him as easily as they once did. The indwelling Holy Spirit is a new and permanent source of strength. Use it and you will become indomitable. Instead of sin having dominion over you, you will gain dominion over it!

Romans 8:26 shows us how to loose that power on the inside of us as never before:

Likewise the Spirit also helpeth our infirmities: for
we know not what we should pray for as we ought:
but the Spirit itself maketh intercession for us with
groanings which cannot be uttered.

These "groanings" can also be interpreted as strong crying and tears. The Holy Spirit prays, groans, and cries through you and breaks the hold of any hindrances standing in the way of God's perfect will for your life. Continue to pray like that and allow the Holy Spirit to have His way in you. The root of those desires will start to fade away and the bad fruit will just naturally fall off the tree. Again, this is not a matter of self-reliance; relying on your own will to change your weaknesses can take you only so far. Only through the Spirit can you mortify the deeds of the body.

Even the famous 20th century British evangelist Smith Wigglesworth said, "The day will come when we will consider nothing as our own, because we will be so taken up with the Lord. The church will ripen into coming glory."

Born in England in 1859, Wigglesworth was a simple but remarkable man whom the Lord used in an extraordinary way. Thousands came to the Lord, were filled with the Spirit, and miraculously healed through his ministry. The Holy Spirit used Wigglesworth to preach the Gospel worldwide. He was not baptized in the Holy Spirit until the age of 48, but once he was, he "had a new power that enabled him to preach, and even his wife was amazed at the transformation."[6]

Wigglesworth said that reading the Word and letting it judge you is the best way to clean yourself up after you repent:

There is a deep secret concerning the imparting of life that involves the believer: "Everyone who has this hope in Him purifies himself, just as He

is pure" (1 John 3:3). There is a lovely passage
along this line in 1 Corinthians 11:31-32: "If we
would judge ourselves, we would not be judged.
But when we are judged, we are chastened by
the Lord, that we many not be condemned with
the world."[7]

Charles Parham, considered the leader of the outpouring of
the Holy Spirit at the beginning of the 20th century, would stress
the importance of repentance in his messages with dramatic
results. One young man who was dramatically converted was an
athlete named Howard Goss. The captain of a professional football team, Goss ran 12 miles every morning to keep in shape.
He was far from being a Christian.

> Neither he or his brothers attended Sunday school
> or church or read the Bible. His brother John was
> an infidel and he passed around such authors as
> Paine, Voltaire, Ingersoll and others. Howard was
> strongly affected by these atheistic teachings.
>
> This was the state of things with Howard
> Goss when Charles Parham came to town with
> his revolutionary teachings. The stir that followed
> naturally attracted his attention.[8]

Howard began attending Parham's meetings. After watching
miracles take place, he became convinced there was a God. But
it was the Baptism of the Holy Spirit that finally convinced Goss
to repent and give his life to God.

Goss described Parham's ministry with the following words:

> I remember well Brother Parham's preaching.
> Himself a personable, gifted, accomplished

original and forceful thinker and a vivid, mag-
netic personality with superb, versatile platform
ability, he always held his audience in the curve
of his hand.

People sat spellbound, one moment weeping,
the next rocking with laughter, as the words
flowed from his lips like water gushing from a
fountain. But through it all he was sending home
with clean, incisive, powerful strokes, the unadul-
terated Word of God.

His humility, his meekness and his consecra-
tion impressed everyone most favorably, and he
became a father to us all. He took the Word of
God literally and practiced it as such, teaching us
that each command Jesus ever gave should be literally obeyed at any cost. Prevailing prayer solved
every problem, and it was the foundation of all
his work.[9]

The Lord talked to Goss about going into the ministry
but he did not respond quickly. Then one Sunday morning he
had a serious accident. A horse kicked him in the face, injur-
ing his eye and tearing his jaw open. As he lost conscious-
ness, he heard a voice saying, "This is your last chance." He
answered, "Yes, Lord, I'll go." The church prayed for him and
he was totally healed. Goss later became the leader of a large
Full Gospel denomination.[10]

Even ministers who have seen the power of God sometimes
need to repent of unbelief when sickness hits their own lives.
Among them was Raymond T. Richey as he served as associate
Pastor for his father, E.N. Richey, at the Gospel Tabernacle in
Houston, Texas, during the First World War. He ministered
to the sick and dying soldiers at Camp Logan, near Houston,

preaching the Gospel to them daily for months. He finally came down with a potentially fatal disease himself. The best army specialists were consulted and they confirmed the diagnosis to him.

> "Richey, you have tuberculosis. Your chance is a slim one. Go to California for a year and take a rest cure. Read nothing, not even the Bible. This may help you; we cannot be sure. Certain it is, that you will live only a short time if you do not do this."
>
> Richey lay in bed discouraged, but the Lord reminded him of healings that had already taken place in his family. Repentant and broken he whispered back, "Dear Lord forgive me; I do remember and I do believe." Reaching for his Bible he opened to Psalm 103 and he read the third verse: "Who forgiveth all thine iniquities; who healeth all thy diseases." Pushing back the covers he raised up in bed. The devil was trying to discourage him, but he knew God had spoken and he was believing for victory in his body. His strength came rapidly and he knew he was healed. This was in September 1919, and after that time he was in meetings almost continually.[11]

Even ministers can get filled with the Spirit and go on to greater glory. Charles S. Price was a Methodist pastor in Spokane, Washington. He worked with the Free Methodist Mission and practiced the doctrine of scriptural holiness. He was asked early on in his ministry to be filled with the Spirit, but refused after another minister told him it would wreck his future and his life. Price yielded to this man's voice instead of the voice of the Holy Spirit.

"That was the turning point of my life. ...I foolishly turned my back on the Cross and started along the trail that led to the labyrinth of modernism. I very soon got to the point where I could explain every religious emotion from the standpoint of psychology. ...I never gave an altar call—never led a soul to Jesus—never preached the glory of the born-again experience. I was spiritually blind, leading my people into the ditch."

The years went by and eventually Price found himself pastoring in Lodi, California. Then a revival broke out with six thousand people attending nightly in nearby San Jose, CA. Price was encouraged to go, and commented, "It was not the sermon that convinced me that night, half so much as the altar. The altar literally filled with people. A mechanic near me got saved and, at the very top of his lungs, shouted, 'Hallelujah, I'm saved, isn't that wonderful? Isn't it glorious, Mr. Price?' I tried to conceal my embarrassment because of the noise that he was making. The best I could do was to say, 'Yes, brother, stick to it, stick to it'—and I got out of the tent as fast as I could."

But the Lord continued to deal with him all night long. The next night the message from the evangelist punctured his modernistic theology "until it looked like a sieve." Arriving back at his hotel room, he threw himself on his knees and cried out to God, and promised he would change. The very next night Price was filled with the Spirit and prayed for hours at the altar. His life and ministry was dramatically changed.[12]

SUMMARY

1. Replace any negative thought patterns with positive ones. This will cause a domino effect that will improve your circumstances over time.

2. Develop a sense of the Presence of the Lamb of God and you will want to be used by Him to reach the lost.

3. Be careful to recognize that you can never know the full magnitude of your salvation. That realization will help you to be grateful to God.

4. Once you are filled with the Holy Spirit with the evidence of speaking in tongues, be faithful to *use* the gift He has given you.

5. You cannot break bad habits through the strength of your own will. The Holy Spirit living inside of you is the agent of change.

CHAPTER SEVEN

CRY FOR YOUR
CHILDREN

S top and let God cry through you! Yield and you will see things differently. Crying is an ingredient you can add to your prayer life. *"... Weeping may endure for a night, but **joy cometh** in the morning"* (Ps. 30:5, emphasis added).

God wants us to be fruitful as well as intimate in prayer with Him. We have tried to hide the fact that we are spiritually barren by making excuses for our lack of fruitfulness in prayer.

A CRY TO HAVE CHILDREN

Hannah was the mother of Samuel; he became one of the greatest prophets in the Old Testament. Before Samuel was born, Hannah was desperate to break the curse of barrenness on her life. That curse would be broken, but her firstborn, Samuel, would not be conceived without a struggle.

The enemy would rather Samuel had never been born, since Samuel was the prophet who would anoint David to become king in place of Saul. David's role was significant; he was in the lineage of Jesus and had a heart of forgiveness that foreshadowed Christ's coming.

Hannah's husband Elkanah had two wives—Hannah and Peninnah. He loved Hannah dearly and wanted to give her a child. When Hannah did not get pregnant, Elkanah gave her a double portion of what he gave Peninnah, *"...for he loved Hannah: although the Lord had closed her womb"* (1 Sam. 1:5 NKJV).

In those days, barrenness brought shame to women. To make matters worse, Peninnah was jealous of Elkanah's affection for Hannah and went out of her way to make fun of her. *"And* [Hannah's] *rival also provoked her severely, to make her miserable, because the Lord had closed her womb"* (1 Sam. 1:6 NKJV). Peninnah probably plied Hannah with many taunting remarks, gloating over her many children.

Hannah's trial was not over in a short period of time. Her barrenness went on for years! Penninah even tormented Hannah when she went to the temple, a place where Hannah went to hear from the Lord and get some peace. *"So it was, year by year, when she went up to the house of the Lord, that she provoked her; therefore she wept and did not eat"* (1 Sam. 1:7 NKJV).

The story of Hannah and Peninnah echoes that of Rachel and Leah. Rachel was barren, while her sister, Leah, conceived easily. Like Hannah, Rachel was desperate to have a child of her own: *"When Rachel saw that she bare Jacob no children, Rachel envied her sister; and said unto Jacob, Give me children, or else I die"* (Gen. 30:1).

There was a cry in Rachel's heart for a child. Hannah knew that cry. She poured out her heart to God. Elkanah

noticed her crying and said, *"Hannah, why do you weep?...
And why is your heart grieved? Am I not better to you than ten
sons?"* (1 Sam. 1:8 NKJV).

Elkanah's affection for and intimacy with Hannah was great,
but she wanted more. She was desperate for a child. His love was
not enough; she had to be fruitful. So Hannah had to go a little
deeper and lay it all out to the Lord:

> *And she was in bitterness of soul, and prayed to
> the Lord and wept in anguish. Then she made a
> vow and said, "O Lord of Hosts, if You will indeed
> look on the affliction of Your maidservant and
> remember me, and not forget Your maidservant,
> but will give Your maidservant a male child, then
> I will give him to the Lord all the days of his life,
> and no razor shall come upon his head"* (1 Samuel
> 1:10-11 NKJV).

Hannah would not let go from crying out to God. She had
to have a harvest. She was intimate with God and that intimacy
led to fruitfulness.

> *So it came to pass in the process of time that
> Hannah conceived and bore a son, and called his
> name Samuel, saying, "Because I have asked for
> him from the Lord"* (1 Samuel 1:20 NKJV).

Even though Hannah was tormented, provoked, bitter, and
in anguish, she would not give way to the ultimate pity party;
she would not just sit there and feel sorry for herself. She rose up
in spite of years of ridicule and cried in anguish to the Lord, even
adding to her prayer a vow, or solemn pledge, to Him regarding
her firstborn.

Penninah's mocking spirit had caused Hannah great pain, but it also provoked her to cry out to God. Sometimes we need to get more desperate before we can begin to move in the right direction. God heard the cry of Hannah's heart and answered her. Consequently, one of the Bible's greatest prophets was born.

A cry will bring miracles. The Western Church can no longer excuse away its lack of miracles, especially when they are so prevalent in third-world countries. These other countries have a cry. They are desperate. Many in Africa will walk for days to get to a healing crusade. Their hearts are ready for a miracle. African Christians do not just show up at a church service and say, "I wonder what this preacher can do for me." They are desperate for God to move and show up wherever He is on display.

Oral Roberts used to say the people who were healed in his early crusades were those who were expecting a miracle the moment he laid hands on them. Roberts relates this story:

> I prayed for a young girl one night in Norfolk, Virginia. She was about eighteen and had been born totally blind. I have not been able to pray the prayer of faith for as many blind people as I want to, but when my faith is right and their faith is right, God heals them. This young girl was brought by her mother into the prayer line. She turned to me and said, "Brother Roberts, put your hand upon my eyes and when you do, God will let me see." I knew this girl meant it. I knew that she had my placing my hand upon her head as a point of contact. I sensed that we were on the verge of a great miracle. I turned to the huge audience and told them what the girl said and asked them to have compassion.

I asked the girl if she had ever seen anything. She said, "No, not even my Mother's face." When she said that, the audience and I cried like children. I have never seen an audience so moved as they were that night. It seemed that the whole crowd was one person. I prayed a short prayer, put my right hand upon her blind eyes and commanded the blindness to go in the name of Jesus Christ of Nazareth. When I did, the presence of God came into my hand and I jerked it back. At that split second she released her faith. Suddenly, the power of God came upon her, she opened her eyes and screamed at the top of her voice, "I can see! I can see!"

Her mother grabbed her and stood looking at her. Then the girl saw her mother's face for the first time. Her hands darted out and she took her mother's face in her hands and looked into her eyes. She began to shout that she could see her mother's face. The crowd leaped up and stood, magnifying and praising God.

I am pointing out these things to you because it is important to know how to be healed. Many are not healed. The reason they are not healed is that they do not understand how to believe right. Then there are some people who want God to heal them regardless of their own believing. To them healing is some kind of magic. You will find the master key to your healing is your own believing.[1]

God wants us to compound the intimacy we experience with Him in His presence and add results for His Kingdom. He wants to take us into a season of crying where we are desperate to see the manifestation. It is a cry of destiny to produce signs and wonders wherever we are, to heal the sick in Wal-Mart, to raise the dead alongside the freeway after a fatal collision, or get people delivered in the middle of a rock concert.

The prophet Joel exhorts us to *"...weep between the porch and the altar..."* (Joel 2:17). There are nations, people, states, and cities reeling from moral decay. Recently we saw a t-shirt in a concert that said "Join me in hell." What that misguided person does not understand is that, first of all, hell is a real place just like Heaven is. Second, he will never see any of his friends in hell; instead, he will be totally alone and tormented with no way of ever getting out. He also does not realize that the screams and the cries of the people there are unlike anywhere else. The only party in hell, if you want to call it that, is the one demons have as they rip your skin and body into shreds over and over again for eternity.

We must walk away from pride and arrogance and everything that keeps us from totally falling on the Rock of our salvation. God wants to grip us with a sense of urgency and desperation. When we feel His heartbeat, we will weep because we will hear the cries of the world and our communities.

My wife, Mary, and I had been married for nearly three years in 1982, however there was no sign of getting pregnant. We were happy to have this time together to start our married life, but after awhile we began to wonder if there was a problem. We had pioneered a new church in Santa Barbara, California, two years before and were raising up a young congregation. Everything was going well; the church was growing and people were getting saved. But anxiety was trying to take hold of us, just as it tried in Hannah's life.

We were ready to start a family, but no fruit was showing. Finally, the Holy Spirit led Mary to cry out at the altar of the church the night before an evangelist was coming to minister. On Sunday morning, when the minister started his meetings, the Lord used him to pray for women who were unable to have children. He had a string of testimonies of women who had come to the altar for just such a prayer and who had subsequently became pregnant during the following months.

Of course, Mary immediately got in the healing line when she heard this. And, after years of barrenness, Mary found out she was pregnant with our first daughter. During an all-night prayer and fasting meeting, she felt so sick she had to run behind the stage curtain and eat some saltines. Mary thought she had food poisoning. But what was really happening was morning sickness: the very thing she had prayed and cried out to God for.

Our first child was on its way. A prophecy from a pastor during the pregnancy said that this would be a miracle birth. We thought that was unusual, because the conception itself had been miraculous. But when our first daughter, Angela Ann, was born, it turned out that a Caesarean section was necessary. The obstetrician was a Christian whose mother was Spirit-filled and had been praying for him to receive the Baptism. This doctor needed to see a miracle. Even he remarked that Angela Ann's birth was from God. He said there was so much scar tissue around the fallopian tubes, he would have given Mary a 10 percent chance of ever having conceived. However, those adhesions did not stop God from answering her cry for a child.

CRY ON BEHALF OF YOUR CHILDREN

Once you have a child, you may have new reasons to cry out to God. The Word assures you that if you *"train up a child in the way he should go . . . he will not depart from it"* (Prov. 22:6)—even when he gets old.

Even when you see your children—the ones whom you have so lovingly led through the Scriptures, taken to church, sent to summer camp, and taken on mission trips—turn away from God and follow after the world, that is not the end of their salvation. If you hold onto the Word, He will never fail you nor forsake you. But use your voice; it is the instrument by which you address the issue in the Spirit.

> *Hear a just cause, O Lord, attend to my cry; give ear to my prayer which is not from deceitful lips. Let my vindication come from Your presence...* (Psalm 17:1-2 NKJV).

Never give up on God. No matter how bad it looks with your children, know that He is faithful. Don't give up on them no matter what. But do get determined in your prayer life. Speak the Word about your children to the devil and don't back down. Don't talk to God about your problem: talk to your problem about your God! If you don't, your children may never make it to Heaven. Satan wants you to think God does not hear you, but remember, satan is a thief and a liar. God hears your intercession; Jesus is pleading your case right now before the Father.

The main thing the enemy wants you to do is to waiver in your stand of faith. Instead of a passionate heartfelt prayer, he would rather you go back to lukewarm Christianity. A wavering heart does not please God; your faith is what pleases Him. And don't let the enemy condemn you into thinking, "I am a failure as a Christian. I might as well quit." No, that is exactly what he wants you to do.

Remember that what the devil has meant for harm, God will turn around for good. His eyes *"run to and fro throughout the whole earth, to shew Himself strong in the behalf of them whose heart is perfect toward him...*" (2 Chron. 16:9). You have to remember Jesus died that you might be made righteous and it does not matter what your children, husband, wife, uncle, or aunt are doing right now, He died for you. Stand up for Him! Make the devil sorry he ever messed with your family. Do not back down.

The thing is, if your children have never known the Lord, they do not know they are lost. Their eyes are blinded to the glorious Gospel of truth. Or if they are backslidden, they are now walking in a dark room instead of in the light. Have you ever entered a pitch-black room and groped around for the light switch? Can you remember how your fingers searched to find that plastic plate on either side of the door, or even on the wall outside the room?

Backslidden children get into such darkness that their eyes get used to it. They do not even realize they are in darkness. The devil wants them to get comfortable with it so they think it is okay to live that way. And all the while they are trying to sweep the Holy Spirit into the back of their minds, attempting to ignore the obvious. Meanwhile, the enemy is destroying, killing, and stealing from their lives.

When you stand in the gap for your children and plead your case to God, you provide the spiritual strength the spiritually weakened person needs to come to God. *"I sought for a man among them, that should make up the hedge, and stand in the gap before Me"* (Ezek. 22:30). The weak person cannot do it himself because his faith is not up to it. You are the one God is relying upon to make up the difference. You are their bridge over troubled waters. *"...Even one who is not innocent...will be delivered through the cleanness of your hands"* (Job 22:28).

Norvel Hayes is a well-known national minister whose daughter, Zona, was backslidden for several years. His book, *Stand in the Gap for Your Children*, is a classic. Norvel relates how God told him to love his daughter more. He was traveling on his way to Tulsa, Oklahoma, when the Spirit of God spoke to him. The following conversation and observation ensued:

> "The things you love the most on earth will not come to pass as long as you continue living and praying under your present conditions. There is something more you need to know."
>
> "What is it, Jesus?"
>
> "Your daughter is in so much darkness and her faith is so weak that she will never be able to get out of that darkness. Her faith is too weak for Me to bring My power to her to break that darkness, but your faith has been wavering and it won't work."
>
> "Where has my faith been wavering, Jesus?"
>
> "You have been wondering why I don't hurry up and do it," He said. "I have to be pleased with your faith before I can do what you are asking. Stand in the gap for our daughter with an unwavering faith, and I will come to her. I will manifest Myself to her."
>
> "Beside that," the Lord said, "you haven't been loving her right. When Zona comes in at one or two o'clock in the morning, you haven't been reaching out to her when she comes in. I want you to tell her how much you love her."
>
> I was the one who had to change. I began to watch my mouth and stand with an unwavering faith.[2]

Norvel had to refuse to let his faith waver. He would watch his daughter drive off to the nightclubs in a miniskirt. While she did that, he would tell the devil, saying, "I won't let you have her. You can't have her. You are not going to kill her."[3]

Norvel would also stay in communication with the Lord, saying, "Thank you, Jesus, for bringing Zona back to the Kingdom of God."[4] Norvel wrote: "I just kept thanking and praising God that Zona was coming back into the family of God."[5]

Finally, Zona, and later her husband, Bobby, got gloriously saved in one of Kenneth E. Hagin's meetings at Norvel's church in Cleveland, Tennessee. Zona now pastors her dad's church and is a nationally known minister.

The key to your children's salvation is your staying strong in God.

THE RIGHTEOUS CRY

Remember that Abraham had to take a stand at the age of 100 and had to believe Him in an impossible situation. It was not really a time in his life where he could believe in the natural he was going to be a father, *much less* a father of many nations.

> *As it is written: "I have made you a father of many nations." He is our father in the sight of God, in whom he believed—the God who gives life to the dead and calls things that are not as though they were* (Romans 4:17 NIV).

You know that when Abraham grew strong in faith, *"and gave glory to God,"* (Rom. 4:20 NIV), he was crying out for the manifestation of this child. Abraham was *"fully persuaded"* (Rom. 4:21 NIV), that what God had promised to him, He was able to perform.

Abraham kept his eyes on God and His promise. When you

get discouraged, you take your eyes off Jesus and put them on the problem in front of you. You allow courage to drain out of you by looking at the wrong picture.

In the natural, Abraham faced insurmountable odds. He was believing to have a child with his wife, Sarah, who was 90 years old! Abraham and Sarah were some 50 years past the normal childbearing time.

Yet, God's promise came to pass. Abraham took a stand and would not be swayed from that stand. Instead, he praised and thanked and gave God glory in the midst of his wife's barren condition. This action of praising, worshiping, and glorifying God was what gave them the miracle they needed to make Sarah's womb fruitful.

The Message Bible says:

> *Blessed are the people who know the passwords of praise, who shout on parade in the bright presence of God. Delighted, they dance all day long; they know who You are, what You do—they can't keep it quiet! Your vibrant beauty has gotten inside us...* (Psalm 89:15-17 TM).

The Lord hears the cry of the righteous and delivers them from all of their troubles.

> *The eyes of the Lord are upon the righteous, and His ears are open unto their cry. The righteous cry, and the Lord heareth, and delivereth them out of all their troubles* (Psalm 34:15,17).

You are righteous by virtue of being a child of God, and you are eligible for this promise. It is amazing how much compassion God has for you. If you get into trouble, all you have to do is cry out to God and He will deliver you. He is always there for you. He watches over His Word to perform it (see Jer. 1:12).

When you are believing for your child to come home, don't get into the details of when or how; just believe that what God says in His Word is true and He is bringing your child back to Himself. Analyzing the situation only complicates it and second-guesses God.

Never forget the simplicity that is in Christ Jesus. The Word will speak to you in the midnight hour and remind you that *"...the battle is not yours but God's"* (2 Chron. 20:15). When you wake up thinking about one of your children, it is the Holy Spirit speaking to you. He is alerting you to take authority over the enemy and pray for protection, safety, deliverance, or whatever is laid upon your heart.

However, trusting the Lord means just that: leaving your situation at His feet and going on to the next project. That next assignment is to take your eyes off the problems that would distract you and put your eyes on the answer.

Job went through horrific trials, but it was when he prayed for his friends that he was delivered (see Job 42:10). Are you going to allow God to turn your stony heart into a heart of flesh? He wants to deal with your heart and soften it into a compassionate one, one that will start putting others first, ahead of yourself.

> *I will give them an undivided heart and put a new spirit in them; I will remove from them their heart of stone and give them a heart of flesh* (Ezekiel 11:19 NIV).

Your heart must become the place inside which He can place His own heart for a lost and dying world. We develop a stony heart, like a wall, to protect ourselves from getting hurt. But even Jesus wept. *"And when he was come near, he beheld the city, and wept over it"* (Luke 19:41). The word *wept* here is *klaio* in the Greek, referring to "hard crying, lamentation, and bewailing."[6]

Jesus was profoundly grieved by what was before Him. He saw beyond the facade of the city and was moved with compassion for the lost people the city contained. We need to look behind the facades in our own society and be moved as Jesus was.

For instance, when you see kids at a concert who are tattooed, pierced, and using language that magnifies the worst demonic images out there, it should make anyone with a heart for God weep with compassion. Teenagers need the love of a caring person. If parents aren't there, they will find it elsewhere.

Teenagers have a cry; it might not be as obvious, but it is still loud and deep. We need to wake up to that cry and hear the heart of God in it. We must start to pray and ask God to reveal His heart to us. When we do, the Holy Spirit will create a new dream in our hearts and a whole new compassion for the lost. When you see lost humanity parading in front of you and you follow the burden that wells up from deep inside, then you are following Him. And because God is love, miracles will follow.

To see God restore the broken hearts of our youth, we must cry for this generation.

> *The hearts of the people cry out to the Lord. O wall of the Daughter of Zion, let your tears flow like a river day and night; give yourself no relief, your eyes no rest. Arise, cry out in the night, as the watches of the night begin; pour out your heart like water in the presence of the Lord. Lift up your hands to Him for the lives of your children, who faint from hunger at the head of every street* (Lamentations 2:18-19 NIV).

Let your heart flow like a river in intercession for these youths. They do not understand what they are doing when they are following the crowd. Many are being led by their fleshly impulses. But you see it; let your heart pour forth and make a bridge between them and God. He has given you this authority; now it is a responsibility.

You see things that they do which are not right; instead of judging and criticizing them, take it to your prayer closet, discuss it with the Lord, and send forth the angels to bring effective Christian laborers across their paths. You have more power here on earth than you think. But you have to put it to work. A key in your hand will unlock the door, but you have to put it into the lock and turn the tumblers for the door to actually open. American children are not starving physically, as are children in many other parts of the world; but multitudes are starving emotionally and spiritually. That is where your cry makes the difference.

You are not just crying out for where they are now, but you are crying for the next generation of fathers, mothers, teachers, doctors, lawyers, politicians, newscasters, soldiers, police, farmers, computer technicians, engineers, presidents, prime ministers, and preachers.

It is the anointing that breaks every yoke. When you cry out to the Lord, yokes of bondage begin to drop off people's necks. Times of deliverance will come from your prayers. Imagine people walking out of drug, alcohol, and sexual addictions into a world of joy and freedom in Christ Jesus!

The Lord will give you specific prayer assignments to complete. You will sense that you have prayed them through when you have a note of praise in your heart. We have a responsibility to do this. No amount of psychiatry or psychology, no number of talk shows or cults can come close to substituting for a heartfelt, burden-breaking cry from the heart for this generation. It may not be convenient or comfortable, but it is an assignment from the Lord that He wants you to complete.

"...*My spirit [by the Holy Spirit within me] prays...*" (1 Cor. 14:14 AMP). "...*We know not what we should pray for as we ought...*" (Rom. 8:26), but the Holy Spirit does know and He will guide us every step of the way. Yet, that doesn't mean He will do it *for* us. We have to cooperate with Him.

God is not responsible for your prayer life; the Bible says that you are. He will lead you as to when to pray in your understanding, when to pray in the Spirit, when to cry, and when to groan. He will help you pray in these ways because some things just cannot be expressed in words. Crying and groaning are inspired by the Holy Spirit; they come out of your spirit flowing from His promptings, whether you are praying for yourself or interceding in prayer for others.

There is the prayer of intercession, but there is also a ministry of intercession. In the former, you might be praying for a particular individual at a particular time. If you have a ministry of intercession you might be under the leadership of a pastor, praying for the church at appointed times.

Either way, do not be afraid to yield to intercession when it comes on you. Intercession does not originate in your mind; it comes from your spirit. The Holy Spirit will lead and guide you into intercession; all you have to do is follow Him. He will never lead you to do something that is not edifying.

When you are prompted to pray, begin by praying in the Spirit. Whether you have revelation as to the subject of prayer or not, keep praying. As long as you have the unction to pray, follow that leading until you reach a note of praise.

CRY OUT FOR YOUR VICTORY

In Second Kings 6:28-7:1, there was a great famine in

Samaria. It was so bad, it was to the point where people were eating donkey heads and dove dung and even boiling their own sons for food. The king of Samaria was in great distress, wailing and tearing his clothes for the things he saw and the reports he heard. Then all of a sudden, the prophet Elisha came on the scene saying, *"...Hear ye the word of the Lord..."* (2 Kings 7:1).

You have a choice: you can listen to the report of God's delivering power or you can stand by disdainfully, in a bad situation, with an unbelieving heart. Elisha chose the former. He declared the whole situation would change in 24 hours, but even then, one of the king's officers mocked him and refused to believe his report. What the officer did not realize was that he was not coming against the man, Elisha; he was coming against a word from God Himself. His sarcastic remark—*"Behold, if the LORD would make windows in heaven, might this thing be?"* (2 Kings 7:2)—was countered by further prophetic declaration from Elisha: *"Behold, thou shalt see it with thine eyes, but shalt not eat thereof"* (2 Kings 7:2). And this is exactly what happened at the end of that chapter.

What a word of hope Elisha brought into a desperate situation! God always has a prophetic indicator to your way of escape, if you keep yourself tuned to His channel. Think about the servant who kept going out to look for the cloud in the midst of the drought in obedience to his master, Elijah. He had to keep going seven times until he saw even the smallest indication of rain.

> *And it came to pass at the seventh time, that he said, Behold, there ariseth a little cloud out of the sea, like a man's hand. And he* [Elijah] *said, Go up, say unto Ahab, Prepare thy chariot, and get thee down, that the rain stop thee not* (1 Kings 18:44).

Elijah recognized this as the sign that God had been talking to him about, an indication of imminent rain. Elijah was not going to let the servant give up. He kept sending him out in spite of the fact that he saw nothing on the horizon. That little puff of a cloud was the sign the servant needed from God that rain was on the way.

That may be your situation today, but do not give up. Help is on the way; just keep expecting and believing in His faithfulness to answer prayer.

In Second Kings 7:3, when the four lepers cried out at the Gate of Samaria, *"Why sit we here until we die?"* they were actually crying out for their deliverance and ultimate freedom. Even though those lepers could not see any help from the other side, they were quickened in their spirits to follow the leading of the Lord.

Sometimes we have to take our faith and get aggressive with the devil. He, like any other enemy, does not understand passivity or compromise. He sees it as weakness and takes it as an opportunity to put more pressure on you.

But when you get tough and start making some declarations and decrees, that is when you will start to see him back off. As Job 22:28 states: *"Thou shalt also decree a thing…and the light shall shine upon your ways."* The lepers made up their minds they were not going to sit idly by and just die in the way. No! They were going to get up and do something about their situation, even if it meant going into the enemy's camp. In the natural, that may seem like a strange way to go for deliverance, but sometimes God tells you to zig when it looks like the "natural" way out is to zag.

The lepers left town for the Syrian camp at twilight. Twilight is a time when the sun is very low in the sky and light is dim. Sometimes God requires you to get up and get going even when you cannot see clearly in front of you. But the lepers had made a declaration to change their situation and not let the circumstances control them.

What about you? Are you bold enough to speak your vision into existence and stick by what you said—even if it takes years to come to pass? *"... Though* [the vision] *tarry, wait for it..."* (Hab. 2:3). If it is a vision God has given you, He will bring it to pass.

He did it for the lepers! When they arrived at the Syrian camp (where they thought they would be taken captive), it was deserted! The Syrian army had heard what they thought was a sound of war, the sound of two approaching armies, and they fled for their lives.

Everything starts with a sound! Your salvation started with your confession; you had to open your mouth and ask Jesus into your heart as your personal Lord and Savior. Your confession cannot just be in your thinking; it must be spoken aloud and it will change your life and your body forever.

When you speak the Word of God you bring life to the printed page. Your spirit grabs onto His Word and is nurtured and encouraged by it. Your spirit readily believes your voice, because it has heard your voice longer than any other.

SUMMARY

1. God wants us to be fruitful in prayer and intimate with Him. If your prayers are unfruitful, ask God why and avoid excusing away any unresolved issues.

2. When you're desperate for your prayer to be answered, do what Hannah did; go deeper with God and lay the issue out before Him.

3. No matter how bad things may seem to be with your children, don't give up on them. God is faithful—cry out to Him!

4. You are righteous by virtue of being a child of God. Therefore, you are eligible for His promises.

5. You always have a choice: to cleave to the report of God's delivering power or to surrender to adversity through unbelief.

CHAPTER EIGHT

THE BLOOD
CRIES OUT

Lester Sumrall was an internationally known minister who studied under Smith Wigglesworth. Sumrall had a television ministry out of South Bend, Indiana. This ministry still broadcasts worldwide today. He often had great victories in deliverance using the Blood.

Once, early on in his ministry, he was praying for deliverance for a woman in a Philippine prison. She had been bitten by devils. The woman was a simple villager who spoke only her native language. However, the demon attacking her spoke through her in perfect English!

As Sumrall was praying for her, the demon "first cursed the Father, then the Son, then the Holy Ghost and then the Blood of Jesus, in this order."[1] Sumrall explained that "it almost seemed that the demon believed the Blood of Jesus was alive, the way he cursed it."[2]

In his book *The Power of the Blood,* H.A. Maxwell Whyte writes:

> Remembering that the life of God is in the Blood of Jesus, we are not surprised at the reaction of this strong demon spirit. As soon as any Christian takes the precious Blood of Jesus on his tongue and sings it, talks, or pleads it, the devil gets terribly disturbed.[3]

Once the Blood of Jesus starts coming out of your mouth, he must back off. The Blood says something to God.

Throughout the Bible it is evident that shed blood speaks to God:

> *Now Cain talked with Abel his brother; and it came to pass, when they were in the field, that Cain rose up against Abel his brother and killed him. Then the Lord said to Cain, "Where is Abel your brother?" He said, "I do not know. Am I my brother's keeper?" And He said, "What have you done? The voice of your brother's blood cries out to Me from the ground"* (Genesis 4:8-10 NKJV).

That is the difference between Old Testament legalism and New Testament grace. This is what the Scripture that says, *"…the blood of sprinkling, that speaks better things than that of Abel"* (Heb. 12:24 NKJV) is talking about. The High Priest went into the Holy of Holies once a year to sprinkle the mercy seat with the blood of bulls and goats. This was an annual atonement that had to continue year after year, because the blood of animals lacked eternal value. The animals sacrificed represented significant value to the people, because they came from the people's livelihood, but the atonement purchased by these sacrifices was not lasting.

That is why we have a more perfect sacrifice today in the death, burial, and resurrection of Jesus. His Blood *is* enough. It is the final sacrifice; it covered all sin.

The High Priest had faith that the blood would atone for Israel's sins. Still, simply believing it would not get the job done; he had to *use* the blood. The same is true today. Without the Blood of Jesus, we could not have entered the holy place (which is now within us). Still, we must plead the Blood.

> *Having therefore, brethren, boldness to enter into the holiest by the blood of Jesus, by a new and living way, which He has consecrated for us, through the veil, that is to say His flesh; and having an high priest over the house of God; let us draw near with a true heart in full assurance of faith, having our hearts sprinkled from an evil conscience...* (Hebrews 10:19-22). KJV

If the High Priest had tried to enter the Holy of Holies without pleading the blood, he would have been stricken dead. So he was careful to offer nothing but the blood.[4]

When you plead the Blood of Jesus today, it is immediately effective. However, we don't face the stringent legal requirements the Old Testament priesthood did. We are under a new and better covenant called the *New Testament*. Under this covenant, Jesus became the final sacrifice for us. The Blood still speaks and pleading it demonstrates that we are relying completely on His mercy. The Blood immediately intervenes for us, because it is alive with resurrection power.

Hebrews 12:24 explains:

> *And to Jesus, the Mediator (Go-between, Agent) of a new covenant, and to the sprinkled blood which speaks [of mercy], a better and nobler and more gracious message than the blood of Abel [which cried out for vengeance]* (AMP).

The mercy seat in Heaven is where Jesus is seated with the Father ever interceding for you. That is why it is so important to plead the Blood when you pray.

The whole realm of God's power is open to those who have discovered this secret. All the angels in Heaven come to help and rescue the child of God who honors, uses, and pleads the Blood of Jesus. When you know that the Blood is covering you and your family, you have created a barrier that satan cannot penetrate. The Blood is one substance all the devils in hell cannot come through, but it is not automatic. Your voice must lift it up to Heaven.

Jesus was "*set forth to be a propitiation through faith in His blood....*" (Rom. 3:25). When you audibly plead His Blood, you are exercising faith in that Blood. It should be done in simple believing faith for it to avail, without any trace of fear.[5]

Maxwell Whyte talks about a terrible accident in his home that was turned around for good when his wife applied the Blood. When his third son was a baby, his wife was fixing him hot gruel (porridge) to eat. When going upstairs with the gruel and a jug of boiling water, she tripped and the boiling hot gruel spilled onto her arm. She plead the Blood of Jesus and by the next morning no trace of the burn was noticible.[6]

Pleading the Blood causes confusion in the enemy's camp. It has a primary place in all intercessory prayer. But there will be persecution from those who oppose it. When you plead or sing about the Blood, you are actually bringing the life of God into your worship because the life of Jesus is in the Blood.

When you plead the Blood out loud, always do it in simple believing faith. Whyte's book talks about a naturopathic doctor who contracted ptomaine poisoning.

> He placed his hands upon his own body, and for twenty minutes pleaded the Blood of Jesus, saying, "I plead the Blood of Jesus," over and over again. The result of this attack upon satan's effort to destroy him was that he was completely healed.[7]

Deliverance is always available when you plead the Blood. The Israelites used animal blood in Egypt and it brought them out of bondage (see Exod. 12:22-23); Rahab in Jericho used the blood-line as a signal to Joshua and his army to rescue her when the walls came down (see Josh. 2:18,21). It saved her life and put her in the lineage of Jesus; the high priests of the Old Testament sprinkled blood and it brought forgiveness to the people; Jesus sprinkled His own Blood and it brought forgiveness to all mankind.

Physically the Old Testament priest would take a hyssop branch and dip it into the blood. Then they would sprinkle it on to the lintels of the Israelites' doorposts. But in the Spirit today we use the Blood by faith when we speak it. Speaking and pleading the Blood are really forms of intense intercessory prayer.

The more you plead the Blood, the more power you are bringing to bear on the situation. You do of course want to avoid mechanical repetition; doing this by rote is ineffective and foolish. But when you plead the Blood in faith, it will quickly bring great results. "As New Testament believers-priests, we are to take the living Blood of Jesus and 'sprinkle' it with our tongues before the Lord by repeating the word 'Blood.'"[8]

That will immediately bring satan's work to a halt and nullify his actions.

Think about it, the blood that circulates in your body so many times a minute carries your very life. Naturally, you cannot plead the Blood all the time. But when you face a situation in which you sense the enemy is on the attack or you need special protection, that is your moment to use it as a weapon. Every time you do that you are reminding the Lord of His promises and you are trusting in His mercy. You are also reminding satan that he cannot touch you as long as you are under the Blood.

The enemy works overtime to take the very mention of the Blood out of churches. If there is no Blood disinfectant in the Body of Christ, then demons are free to continue their deadly work to destroy spirit, soul, and body.

TESTING, PROTECTIVE POWER OF THE BLOOD

The Blood has great testing power as well. A person who is bound by the enemy will find it almost impossible to plead the Blood.

This mighty weapon also affords you great protection throughout life. There are many testimonies of people who have dared to oppose the enemy through the power of the Blood. Maxwell Whyte's book relates the story about when he had taken 14 young people skating on a lake in Ontario, Canada. As his car slid on an icy road, he pleaded the Blood aloud and his car missed hitting a telephone pole head-on. Also during that trip home his wife's car went out of control and was spinning in a circle. She pleaded the Blood out loud and the car came to rest without plunging down a 20-foot bank.

Never hesitate to plead the Blood. When you sense opposition, either physically or emotionally, lift up your voice and use the Blood by faith. Pleading the Blood was an accepted form of prayer and worship in early Pentecost. When it is used today, it continues to be extraordinarily effective. We are truly more than conquerors through the Blood of Jesus.

SUMMARY

1. The Old Covenant required an annual atonement for sin; but Jesus' sacrifice is eternal— He paid for all sin, forever.

2. Plead the Blood of Jesus; it is the means by which we are able to enter the "holy place."

3. Pleading the Blood demonstrates your complete reliance on His mercy. The Blood immediately intervenes, because it is alive with resurrection power.

4. When you plead or sing about the Blood, you bring the life of Jesus into your worship, because the life of Jesus is in the Blood.

5. The Blood is the only effective counteragent to corruption; therefore, the enemy works overtime to discourage its mention in our churches.

CHAPTER NINE

THE CRY
OF AZUSA

Adetermined cry from praying saints of the Azusa Street revival brought about a renewal of the Baptism of the Holy Spirit. Over 600 million Charismatics and Pentecostals today can trace their roots to the revival that began in a Los Angeles mission in 1906.[1]

Their prayers were sincere and effective. *"... The effectual fervent prayer of the righteous man..."* (James 5:16) often has tears accompanying it. God wants sincerity in prayer; He wants to hear your heart. Stand before the Lord and just weep before Him.

> *You number my wanderings; put my tears into Your bottle; are they not in Your book? When I cry out to*

*You, **then** my enemies will turn back; this I know,
because God is for me* (Psalm 56:8-9 NKJV).

So many of us have lost the cry; we have become hardened.
Regaining the cry will soften us and bring back compassion into
our hearts.

The Azusa Revival was powerful, a pivotal time for the Body
of Christ. A shekinah glory cloud filled the Azusa Street warehouse for three-and-a-half years during the outpouring. The
presence of God was thick during those meetings; even 3-year-
olds could sense it. Little Jean Darnell would try to "gather the
mist in her arms"[2] as she woke up from her nap under the pew
where her mother had placed her. Years later, she would understand how she "learned of the miracles and Presence of God in
the form of the shekinah glory—so thick during those meetings—where she found comfort under the pew."[3]

Little Jean would have no idea how God's glory would have
a lifelong affect on her. She became a spiritual giant herself. In
1944 Jean became Pastor Darnell of Angelus Temple. She suc-
ceeded to the pulpit of famed preacher Aimee Semple-McPherson,
the founder of the Four Square denomination.

This mighty woman of God would often relate her stories
about Azusa. Flames were seen over the building when the
greatest miracles were occurring. Firemen were called because
people passing by would see "flames leaping up from the roof
of the building."[4]

Sister Carney was 17 years old when she first arrived at
the Azusa Street mission. One of the few who had received
the Baptism of the Holy Spirit before joining the Azusa Street
mission, Carney was already excited about praying in tongues.
She had already been asked to leave the First Baptist Church of
Pasadena because of her desire to witness to her friends about
the experience of being filled with the Holy Spirit.

Sister Carney would tell of the beginning of this revival that touched the world with an excitement that stayed with her for 60 years. Carney had the ability to relate the Azusa stories in more detail than the others, even decades later.

Once, a neighbor of the mission called the Los Angeles Fire Department to report a fire in the Azusa building. When firefighters arrived, they could smell no smoke nor see any evidence of fire. The reports kept coming however, and Carney walked outside to see the flames for herself.

Lake later had one of the most notable healing ministries of the 20th century.

Afterward, Brother Seymour, the "leader" of the revival, would point to them and say, "Everyone on the cots or wheelchairs, you're healed in the Name of Jesus."[5]

Another faithful Azusa participant was Brother Anderson. This 15-year-old was fascinated by the glory of God that would roll into that building. Anderson said the shekinah glory was hard to explain because...

> ...it could only be described, but not understood. At times, he would come into the building, and there would be kind of a glow. There were times God would start moving and working, and a smoke-like substance would begin to glow even brighter. People would walk through it, and sometimes it would sort of roll. You couldn't take a fan and blow it out, nor was it something you could pick up.[6]

Brother Anderson described the fire that would come down and up from the building of the Azusa Street prayers. He said it looked like flames and how "the burning bush Moses described now made sense."[7]

Anderson said the greatest thing that impressed him was when Brother Seymour started praying in the gifts as the Spirit fell upon him. There were many times where groups of people would come in with rheumatoid arthritis and Seymour would "point to maybe a half dozen of them and say, 'You want to see a miracle over there?' Every one of you within a few minutes are going to be up and walking in the Name of Jesus.' And every one of them—you could hear their bones popping—would be up shouting as their legs and arms and hands straightened out."[8]

Sister Carney was fast friends with two other young men who liked to go around and see everyone healed. C.W. Ward and Ralph Riggs later became the founders and leaders of large denominations, the Assemblies of God and the Church of Christ.

SUMMARY

1. God desires sincerity and transparency of heart in our prayers. When you weep before Him, He hears and listens.

2. Regaining the cry in our hearts will soften us and increase compassion for others.

3. The Azusa Revival was a powerful, pivotal time for the Body of Christ.

4. The Azusa Revival was marked by profound signs and wonders including the appearance of fire and the presence of a glory "cloud."

5. Denominations, such as the Assemblies of God and the Church of Christ, sprang from the Azusa Revival.

CHAPTER TEN

THE CRY
OF REVIVAL

The cry of revival is a spirit of prayer. Charles Finney, the great 19th-century revivalist, had almost entire towns saved in place after place. What was the secret to Finney's success? He was an early riser and would pray for hours every morning. Finney would put the Lord in remembrance of His Word concerning revival and then expect an answer to his prayers.

Finney was persistent, consistent, and prayed the Word of God back to Him. God is always looking for an intercessor, saying, "My eyes roam to and fro across the earth looking for someone to be faithful to" (see 2 Chron. 16:9).

Are you the one He is tapping on the shoulder? Has the Holy Spirit been prompting you to wake up in the middle of the night and pray? If He is calling you to pray, know that He wants to do something great in your life as you intercede in the life of another.

Whether for good or for evil, what you sow—spiritually as well as physically and financially—is what you are going to reap.

DON'T OVERLOOK THE YOUTH

There are only two reasons why a salvation prayer for someone's soul remains unanswered. Either sin or unbelief resides in the heart of the one doing the praying or satan is hindering the answer.

If there is anything you need to clear out of your life before you start praying, figure out what it is and clean it out of your heart. After you have repented of unbelief or any other hindering force, the answer will come. Satan cannot continue to hold out against righteous, bold, fervent prayer.

In Ireland, the great 19th-century revivalist, James McQuilkin, was greatly influenced by the faith of George Mueller. Mueller had literally supported hundreds of orphans daily through much prayer at his Bristol, England, orphanage. McQuilkin was saved in 1856 and soon after that read George Mueller's narratives. Mueller's writings had a great effect on McQuilkin:

> God blessed [the narratives] greatly to [McQuilkin's] soul, especially in showing to him what could be obtained by prayer. He said to himself something like this: 'See what Mr. Mueller obtains simply by prayer. Thus I may obtain blessing by prayer.' He now set himself to pray that the Lord would give him a spiritual companion, one who knew the Lord. Soon after he became acquainted with a young man who was a believer. These two began

a prayer-meeting in one of the Sunday schools in
the parish of Connor. Having his prayer answered
in obtaining a spiritual companion, Mr. James
McQuilkin asked the Lord to lead him to become
acquainted with some more of His hidden ones.
Soon after the Lord gave him two more young
men, who were believers previously, as far as he
could judge."[1]

The four young friends prayed for four months until in
January 1858, a farm hand was converted. He started praying
with them, and another 20-year-old man joined them. Praying
through the year, this group continued converting many.[2]

About Christmas, 1858, a young man...who
had been converted through this little company
of believers, went to see his friends...and spoke
to them about their own souls, and the work
of God [in a certain town]. His friends desired
to see some of these converts. Accordingly Mr.
James McQuilkin, with two of the first who met
for prayer, went on February 2, 1859, and held
a meeting in one of the Presbyterian churches.
Some believed, some mocked, and others thought
there was a great deal of presumption in these
young converts; yet many wished to have another
meeting. This was held...[two weeks later]; and
now the Spirit of God began to work, and to
work mightily. Souls were converted, and from
that time conversions multiplied rapidly. Some of
these converts went to other places, and carried
the spiritual fire, so to speak, to them. The
blessed work of the Spirit of God spread in many

places.... From this time, the work of the Holy Ghost spread further and further; for the young converts were used by the Lord to carry the truth from one place to another.

Such was the beginning of that mighty work of the Holy Spirit, which has led to the conversion of hundreds of thousands; for some of my readers will remember how in 1859 this fire was kindled in England, Wales and Scotland; how it spread through Ireland, England, Wales and Scotland; how the Continent of Europe was more or less partaking of this mighty working of the Holy Spirit; how it led thousands to give themselves to the work of evangelism; and how this work is going on in Europe generally; these facts are stated in order that it may be seen what delight God has in answering abundantly the believing prayer of His children.[3]

STAND YOUR GROUND

Over 130 years ago almost 70 percent of the continent of Europe was saved; today this continent is the darkest landmass in the world—not socially or economically, but spiritually. Only a small percentage of the European population counts themselves as knowing Jesus Christ as their personal Lord and Savior. It is time to cry out for Europe and the United Kingdom again; although there was once a fire of revival, the flames have since died down. It is time to bring it back into the present day.

Smith Wigglesworth came over from England and preached on the public square of Boston, Massachusetts. When he began to speak, people climbed up into the trees to see him because the crowd was so large. Wigglesworth would ask them to climb back down because, when the power of God would come, people would fall out of the trees.

Smith Wigglesworth believed and said that God delights in His children having the audacity of faith to say, "God, you have promised it, so now do it." When faith compels you to say such words to God, you put Him in remembrance of what He said. If the Lord is telling us to put Him in remembrance, then we need to do it.

Whatever you are praying about, fight it out in prayer. You are not fighting against God or people, but against powers and principalities and rulers of this present darkness (see Eph. 6:12). God wants to answer you; He hears your petition the first time you pray it (see Dan. 10:12). But, whenever you are praying something through, there will be warfare in the heavenlies and on earth. It is spiritual warfare against the hosts of darkness.

However, demons cannot stand against the sword of the Spirit, the Word of God, and the mighty Name of Jesus. These are your nuclear weapons, spiritually speaking. If you will pray through to the victory, you can defeat the devil every single time!

Prayer means doing just that: fighting demons who will try to keep your prayers from being answered. Of course, the answers to your prayers will not fall on you like apples from a tree; you must stand your ground. But you must take your place as a believer and not back down concerning your identity in Christ.

Cry out to God, stand on God's Word, and declare what God has told you. Look your storm in the face like Paul did. He describes the scene as he encouraged those who feared a catastrophe:

> *For there stood by me this night the angel of God,*
> *whose I am, and whom I serve, saying, Fear not,*

Paul; thou must be brought before Caesar: and,
lo, God hath given thee all them that sail with
thee. Wherefore, sirs, be of good cheer: for I believe
God, that it shall be even as it was told me
(Acts 27:23-25).

Paul defied the contradictory circumstances in which he found himself. You can do the same! If you do, you will see devils and demons relenting in their opposition; and you will see the answer come. Hold fast with pit bull determination, knowing God hears you.

SUMMARY

1. The cry of revival is a spirit of prayer. Your prayers can stir revival!

2. If God is calling you to pray, He wants to accomplish something great through your intercession.

3. There are only two reasons a salvation prayer remains unanswered. Either there is sin or unbelief in the one doing the praying or satan is hindering the answer.

4. Remember when you are praying that you are not fighting against God or people, but against the powers, principalities, and rulers of this present darkness.

5. Demons cannot stand against the Word of God and the mighty Name of Jesus. These are your nuclear weapons, spiritually speaking.

CHAPTER ELEVEN

CRY FOR YOUR
NATION

G eorge Washington cried out for our nation. Our first president prayed the following:

> Direct my thoughts, words and work. Wash away my sins in the immaculate blood of the lamb, and purge my heart by thy Holy Spirit....Daily frame me more and more into the likeness of thy son, Jesus Christ.[1]

If this country runs into problems, it is not the fault of the president, Congress, or the Pentagon. Christians of this great nation must rise up and cry out to God with heart, purpose, and passion.

External influences will attempt to destroy the very fabric of this nation if we do not cry out. Terrorists are not silent since murdering more than 3,000 people on September 11, 2001. They are continuing to plan their next move. But, if we cry out against wickedness, their plans will be foiled.

Violent crime has invaded American homes and schools, but we can turn it around through passionate prayer. Drugs and alcohol destroy the very fabric of the country, but we can bind up spirits of sorcery and drugs with our heartfelt prayers.

> *If My people, which are called by My name, shall humble themselves, and pray, and seek My face, and turn from their wicked ways; then will I hear from heaven, and will forgive their sin, and will heal their land* (2 Chronicles 7:14).

This is a promise from God: if we humble ourselves (or open ourselves up to God's perfect will) and stop long enough in our busy lives to hear what He is saying, then we will have results. We must pray *and* seek His face. Seeking His face requires a lot more fervor and determination than just an ordinary prayer.

Not only must we humble ourselves, earnestly pray, and seek His face; we must also meet one more requirement before hearing from Heaven: we must turn from our wicked ways.

Our daughter Katy was a prolific songwriter even at a young age. One song, written when she was 13, became a popular radio hit in 2001. The lyrics of "Search Me" touched people's hearts. The words were based on Psalm 139:23-24:

> *Search me, O God, and know my heart; try me, and know my anxieties; and see if there is any wicked way in me, and lead me in the way everlasting* (NKJV).

The psalmist demonstrates the fact that people do want to know what is keeping them from moving forward in God's perfect plan for their lives. We know He always has the answer for us; He just wants us to be passionate in our desire to hear it. The Lord never turns His back on His promises, He just requires us to believe and act on them.

The exciting part is that it does not take an army of people to affect a nation with prayer. Of course, united prayer goes a long way in establishing God's plan on the earth. But Abraham shows how one determined person can impact the world. Abraham interceded so that God would not destroy Sodom and Gomorrah, even if only ten righteous people lived there.

> *And the Lord said, Because the shriek [of the sins] of Sodom and Gomorrah is great and their sin is exceedingly grievous, I will go down now and see whether they have done altogether [as vilely and wickedly] as is the cry of it which has come to Me; and if not, I will know* (Genesis 18:20-21 AMP).

The angels of the Lord proceeded towards Sodom, but Abraham stood before the Lord. He was not giving up even though the decree of destruction was being put into action. At that critical moment, Abraham did not draw back in fear of what the Lord had proposed to do. Instead, he drew closer and asked Him:

> *... Will You destroy the righteous ... together with the wicked? ... Suppose there are in the city fifty righteous; will You destroy the place and not spare it for [the sake of] the fifty righteous in it?* (Genesis 18:23-24 AMP).

Abraham didn't stop there. He continued asking God if He would destroy the place if there were 45 righteous people...or 40...or 30...or 20...or 10. Abraham was pressing God Almighty—and he knew it! But God was listening.

> *Oh, let not the Lord be angry, and I will speak again only this once. Suppose ten [righteous people] shall be found there. And [the Lord] said, I will not destroy it for ten's sake* (Genesis 18:32 AMP).

Abraham was intereceding, not for the wicked people of Sodom and Gomorrah, but for his nephew Lot and Lot's family. Once Abraham's relatives were removed from Sodom; the Lord could do what He wanted, because all the righteous were gone from the city.

The point is that *one* person can make all the difference in prayer. The key here is for Christians to take their stand and plead their case to the Lord. When a born-again believer who knows who he is in Christ boldly comes before the throne of God, his prayers have the power to change the events of history as nothing else can.

Don't give up and walk away from your assignment just because you cannot see how one person can make a difference. If the Lord is prompting you to pray something through, you are the one He knows can get the job done. He doesn't make any mistakes. If we back down from the assignments He gives us, He will be forced to pass them on to others.

THE MIRACLE OF SALERNO

One group in Wales turned the tide of the Second World War during a late night prayer meeting. Rees Howells and his Bible college laid down their lives in prayer to see a victory for

England. They gathered together to seek God around 9:45 p.m. The meeting had a solemn tone from the outset. Howells' voice was "trembling with the burden of his message, and scarcely audible as he said, 'The Lord has burdened me between the meetings with the invasion at Salerno. I believe our men are in great difficulties, and the Lord has told me that unless we can pray through, they are in danger of losing their hold.'" The awe of God settled down upon us for this came as a complete surprise, there having been no official news to this effect on the wireless, and we ourselves having previously had some rejoicing that Italy was at last on the point of being delivered from the Fascist and Nazi tyranny. Before long we were on our knees crying to God for Him to intervene. The Spirit took hold of us and suddenly broke right through in the prayers, and we found ourselves praising and rejoicing, believing God had heard and answered. We could not go on praying any longer, so we rose from our knees and began to sing praises, the Spirit witnessing in all our hearts that God had wrought some miraculous intervention in Italy. The victory was so outstanding that I looked at the clock as we rose to sing. It was at the stroke of 11 p.m.

> We waited to hear the midnight news. The announcer told us in effect exactly what the Director had told us from the Lord—that unless some miracle happened, our troops were in grave danger of losing the beachhead in the morning. This only confirmed to us the guidance of the Spirit, and we were more confident than ever that the victory was certain. The news the next morning was more hopeful, but we eagerly awaited newspaper reports from the Front. We were not disappointed. On Thursday morning one of the daily newspapers displayed a front page

headline: The Miracle of Salerno. The account of the reporter personally at the Front ran, "I was with our advanced troops in the invasion of Salerno on Monday. The enemy artillery was advancing rapidly and with ceaseless firing. The noise was terrible, and it was obvious that unless a miracle happened, our troops could never hold up the advance long enough for the beachhead to be established. Suddenly, for no accountable reason, the firing ceased and the Nazi artillery stopped its advance. A deathly stillness settled on the scene. We were waiting in breathless anticipation, but nothing happened. I looked at my watch—it was eleven o'clock at night. Still we waited, but still nothing happened; and nothing happened all that night, but those hours made all the difference to the invasion. By the morning the beach-head was established."[2]

When the Holy Spirit touches your heart deeply enough to impart a heart cry for the lost, for your city, or for nations, you will have a breakthrough. Think of the toughest, hardest person you know. God can perform heart surgery on them. After all, He turned Saul, a murderous, Christian-killing, blaspheming Roman into the author of two-thirds of the New Testament in one encounter on the road to Damascus!

Don't give up on people just because they look spiritually impenetrable. Actually, the Lord delights in turning around hard cases. There is even more glory in it for Him. So when He whispers in your ear to go and witness to your boss, don't be like Ananias who tried to shirk his responsibility to go and tell Paul about the Holy Spirit. For all you know, your boss just learned that he has cancer. Maybe his wife left him that morning or he discovered that his children are on drugs. He may be more ready to hear about Jesus than you think.

When we pastored our first church in the '80s in Southern California, we took over a large section of a warehouse that faced a parking lot. There were some out buildings on the other side of the lot. These structures housed a rough and tough Hells Angels motorcycle gang. Their reputation was well known throughout the community.

A group of faithful prayer warriors in our church gathered every Tuesday morning to pray for our city, the churches, the state, and the country. Intent on seeing a breakthrough in our area, we had annual statewide prayer meetings and encouraged the congregation to attend 6:00 a.m. prayer meetings and monthly all-night prayer meetings.

That prayer group was not a silent bunch, their voices carried down the 30-foot hall of that church, out the door, across the parking lot, and right into the den of that motorcycle gang. Most of the members were usually still recovering from the escapades of the previous weekend. But the prayers from this group of grandmothers roared across the parking lot and through their clubhouse—with authority from Heaven. After a few months of this, the president of the club came over to see what was going on in the church. Of course the ladies were not going to lose this prime opportunity to win a soul; they immediately proceeded to witness to him.

After a period of time, the Hells Angels leader decided to give his life to the Lord. He had such a thorough heart change that he went on to pastor a church in Bakersfield, California. Thank God for people who will pray with a heart of compassion and refuse to be intimidated.

God has a heart cry for the lost, and He will draw you to a place to pray for the harvest, as these ladies did. When the Holy Spirit touches your heart during these seasons of prayer, you will have a cry.

BIRTHING AND KEEPING A NATION

The United States is a free nation. The majority of our founding Fathers were Christians who put our Constitution and Declaration of Independence together using biblical precepts.

We often overlook the benefits of living in the U.S. But step outside her borders and you will quickly realize the atmosphere of freedom you left behind. When you return to the homeland, you will be ready to kiss the ground you once took for granted.

Why is our nation so special? Because the founding fathers of the United States of America literally cried out to God for a nation in which they could worship God freely. The Puritans had lived under persecution and tyranny in the British Isles; they were determined not to let that happen in this new land. For nearly 240 years, the United States of America has lived and had its laws largely directed by these principles.

Sadly, the tide is turning. Today, the same government that will not allow a 13-year-old girl to have a driver's license, smoke cigarettes, or drink alcohol mandates that this same child must have free access to birth control without her parents' knowledge. Where did these incongruent policies come from? Who makes these laws?

Unfortunately, many of our nation's leaders are godless. Many of our federal judges do not know God and have nothing to do with the Bible—the very book that formed the basis of our founding documents!

Some Christians actually do pray for our national leadership to come to the saving knowledge of Jesus Christ. Thank God for the remnant that is proactive and determined! When we, as Christians, don't like what we see happening around us, we cannot stick our heads in the sand and refuse to have anything to do with government.

We know that, if we leave a child to his own devices, he

will come to folly. The same is true of our government if we stop standing up for righteousness! We need to be more spiritually aggressive than ever. We must speak up for righteous voices in our government and not back down in the face of threats or intimidation. What would our founding fathers say to young teens who are getting government permission to allow them to be sexually promiscuous? Or better yet, what would they say to the government that legislated in favor of such behavior?

If we really believe in the seedtime and harvest principle, then as we sow seed and cry out against governmental corruption, we can expect a decline in the moral decay in our society.

Many abortionists, homosexuals, and environmentalists are looking for somebody to represent them in government who will make it easy for us to slide into sin and away from morality. *"For he who sows to his flesh reap will corruption, but he who sows to the Spirit will of the Spirit reap everlasting life"* (Gal. 6:8 NKJV).

If we fail to stand up against the moral decay of our nation, our children will reap the harvest of our neglect. We must rise up, cry out, and vote for godly leaders, or we will have literally handed over the reins of government to people who couldn't care less about God—people who are only interested in promoting humanism and their own agendas.

Rachel Hickson, a British prayer warrior and Bible teacher, explains how shocking information got her motivated to pray for the largest city in the U.K.

> I remember when God first started speaking to me about the city of London. I had heard a bleak report. I had heard of so many good, anointed men, pastors working in London who were getting weary. ... It was like London was chewing up and spitting out ministry.

I began to respond to God and say, "Lord this is not right. What can we do?" and God began to speak to me and say, "You need to provide a prayer shield for My people in the city, so that their backs are covered; so that they are not open to the onslaught of the enemy, because the enemy does not want to yield the capital city. The capital has authority and power. The enemy wants to retain the seat of government. You've got to learn to pray."

...God told me to go to a prayer center in the countryside, take five people with me and spend three days there with no agenda, just listening to Him. ...By His Holy Spirit's power He allowed us to "feel" some of the pain He felt for the city of London.

...Eventually I cried out, "Lord, ten million people live in this city. How can we possibly do anything for them?" Then the answer came: "Divide the city up into twelve regions like you would slice a piece of cake." We began to do this and the M25 Londonprayernet (www .londonprayer.net) was born. God was revealing His strategy to us.[3]

Hickson goes on to say that every city has a unique strategy of its own. She emphasizes that the strategy for London is different than the strategy for your city.

You as an intercessor must seek for that information and let it motivate you to intercede. When you listen to the Lord and allow the Holy Spirit to guide you along His path, you will have a detailed plan, just as Nehemiah had a plan for rebuilding Jerusalem.

God wants His servants to have a fresh experience with Him, a fresh encounter. If I were to sit down with you today, would you say, "Preacher, my well is dry?" God has opened up the door for you to flow in the river of His glory. You can cry in intercession and start to move in a realm of breakthrough that you never thought possible.

Don't stand still frozen in fear! Start to move, start to oppose the enemy of your soul. You can either live in the Dead Sea or the Red Sea. One is static, the other flows. It is your choice. You can stay where you are in life or you can get going into the plan the Lord has for you.

You are in Jesus because God has made a way for you to know Him. Have a heart full of gratitude for what He has done and what He will do. Cry out to Him and watch your world, and the world around you, start to change.

SUMMARY

1. As Christians, we must rise up and cry out to God for our nation—with heart, purpose, and passion.

2. God promises that if we humble ourselves and stop long enough to hear what He is saying our prayers will be effective.

3. As Abraham's life demonstrates, one determined pray-er can impact the world.

4. Don't give up on those who appear to be spiritually impenetrable; the Lord delights in turning around hard cases.

5. We must stand up against the moral decay of our nation; if we don't, our children will reap the harvest of our neglect.

ENDNOTES

PREFACE

1. Merriam-Webster Online Dictionary. Merriam-Webster Online 2009, s.v. "cry," http://www.merriam-webster.com/dictionary /cry (accessed: January 31, 2009).

2. Dictionary.com. The American Heritage Dictionary of the English Language, Fourth Edition. Houghton Mifflin Company, 2004, s.v. "cry," http://dictionary.reference.com/browse/cry (accessed: January 31, 2009).

3. The ARTFL Project. Webster's Revised Unabridged Dictionary (1913 + 1828), s.v. "cry," http://machaut.uchicago.edu /?action=search&word=cry&resource=Webster%27s&quicksearch =on (accessed: May 3, 2009).

4. Ibid.

5. Ibid.

6. Ibid.

7. Ibid.

CHAPTER ONE
GOD HEARS YOUR CRY

1. Finis Jennings Dake, *Dake's Annotated Reference Bible,* Large Note Ed. (Lawrenceville, GA: Dake Bible Sales, 1981), Exod. 14:6.

2.   Ibid, Exod. 15:8.

3.   Ibid, Ps. 24:3.

4.   John Osteen, *The Divine Flow,* 1st ed. (Houston: John Osteen Publishing, 1978), 16-17.

5.   Dake, Ps. 53:1.

6.   Lawrence O. Richards, *The Zondervan Expository Dictionary of Bible Words* (Grand Rapids: Zondervan, 1985), s.v., "miracle."

CHAPTER THREE
YOUR CRY MATTERS

1.   Finis Jennings Dake, *Dake's Annotated Reference Bible,* Large Note Ed. (Lawrenceville, GA: Dake Bible Sales, 1981), Ps 56:8.

CHAPTER FOUR
YOUR VOICE MUST SPEAK

1.   Finis Jennings Dake, *Dake's Annotated Reference Bible,* Large Note Ed. (Lawrenceville, GA: Dake Bible Sales, 1981), 1 Sam. 17:48.

2.   Biblesoft's New Exhaustive Strong's Numbers and Concordance with Expanded Greek-Hebrew Dictionary. CD-ROM. Biblesoft, Inc. and International Bible Translators, Inc. s.v., "mahar," (4116).

3.   Dake, 1 Sam. 17:48.

4.   Ibid, 1 Sam. 17:49.

5.   George Mueller, *Answers To Prayer* (Chicago: Moody Press, 1990), 11-12.

6.   Ibid, 12-14.

CHAPTER SIX
REPENTANCE BRINGS FREEDOM

1.   Finis Jennings Dake, *Dake's Annotated Reference Bible,* Large Note Ed. (Lawrenceville, GA: Dake Bible Sales, 1981), 1 Cor. 9:27.

2.   Ibid.

3.   Ibid.

4.   Ibid.

5.   Smith Wigglesworth, *Experiencing God's Power Today* (New Kensington, PA: Whitaker House, 2000), 133.

6.   Ibid, 8.

7.   Ibid, 107.

8.   Gordon Lindsay, comp., *They Saw It Happen!* (Dallas: Christ For the Nations, 1980), 11.

9.   Ibid, 11-12.

10.   Ibid, 12.

11.   Ibid, 31.

12.   Ibid, 37-41.

CHAPTER SEVEN
CRY FOR YOUR CHILDREN

1.   Oral Roberts, *Deliverance from Fear and Sickness* (Tulsa: Oral Roberts, 1954), 65-68.

2.   Norvel Hayes and Zona Cornelison, *Stand in the Gap for Your Children* (Tulsa: Harrison House, 1991), 16-18.

3.   Ibid, 17.

4.   Ibid, 18.

5.   Ibid, 18.

6.   Finis Jennings Dake, *Dake's Annotated Reference Bible,* Large Note Ed. (Lawrenceville, GA: Dake Bible Sales, 1981), Luke 19:41.

CHAPTER EIGHT
THE BLOOD CRIES OUT

1.   H.A. Maxwell Whyte, *The Power of the Blood* (New Kensington, PA: Whitaker House, 1973), 29.

2.   Ibid.

3.   Ibid, 30.

4.   Ibid, 32.

5.   Ibid, 74.

6.   Ibid, 52-53.

7.   Ibid, 74.

8.   Ibid.

CHAPTER NINE
THE CRY OF AZUSA

1.   Paul Strand Sr., "The Lasting Impact of the Azusa Street Revival," *CBNNews.com*, http://www.cbn.com/cbnnews/usnews /060424a.aspx (accessed May 5, 2009).

2.   J. Edward Morris, Cindy McCowan, and Tommy Welchel, *They Told Me Their Stories* (Dare2Dream, 2006), 37.

3.   Ibid, 21-22.

4.   Ibid, 37.

5.   Ibid, 55.

6.   Ibid, 49-50.

7.   Ibid.

8.   Ibid, 48.

CHAPTER TEN
THE CRY OF REVIVAL

1.   George Mueller, *Answers To Prayer* (Chicago: Moody Press, 1990), 77.

2.   Ibid, 78.

3.   Ibid, 78-80.

CHAPTER ELEVEN
CRY FOR YOUR NATION

1.   William J. Johnson, *George Washington, The Christian* (New York: The Abingdon Press, 1919), quoted in "George Washington's Prayer Journal," CBN.com, http://www.cbn.com/spirituallife /PrayerAndCounseling/Intercession/washington_prayer.aspx.

2.   Norman P. Grubb, *Rees Howells Intercessor* (Fort Washington, PA: Christian Literature Crusade, 1980) 271-272.

3.   Rachel Hickson, *Supernatural Communication: The Privilege of Prayer* (West Sussex, UK: New Wine Press, 2006), 201-202.

AUTHOR CONTACT
INFORMATION

KEITH HUDSON MINISTRIES

PO Box 891147

Temecula, CA 92589

www.keithhudson.org

wordinaction3@verizon.net

the CRY